In Pursuit of the American Dream

a Tribute To
Dave Ramsey Baby Steppers
Book #1

NANCY GASKINS

Copyright © 2020 Nancy Gaskins

All rights reserved.

ISBN: 9781678605353

DEDICATION

To Dave Ramsey
and the millions of
Ramsey Baby Steppers world-wide
who continue to inspire the world
by sharing your daily financial struggles and
allowing us to celebrate with you
during your triumphs.

Your constant words of encouragement,
advice, honest feedback and
reality checks when we get out of line
is worth more than words can express.

Thank you!

CONTENTS

	Acknowledgments	i
1	Introduction	1
2	It's OK To Be Weird	5
3	Dave's Baby Steps	9
4	Side Hustles & Dave Cars	13
5	When Murphy Comes Knocking	21
6	Where We Invest	23
7	Cash Flowing College	25
8	Mortgage Free	27
9	Give Like No One Else	31
10	Life of a Baby Stepper: Dumb Stuff We've Done With Money - Debt Free Screams - When Murphy Comes Calling - 101 Side Hustles	35

ORDINARY PEOPLE, EXTRAORDINARY LIVES
DO YOU HAVE WHAT IT TAKES?

Are you living beneath your God-given potential? If you are honest, most people would have to answer with an unequivocal, "yes." My objective for this book series is two-fold. First, to give the reader a glimpse inside the daily lives of a group of people whom I have grown to love, admire and respect for their amazing efforts of going against the grain from what the world deems to be "normal," so they can change their family tree for generations to come; the *Ramsey Baby Steppers*.

Every day, *Ramsey Baby Steppers* prove to the world what most people say "can't" be done, CAN be done, and in a shorter time than most could ever deem possible. Getting your personal finances in order and building a strong, solid financial foundation is the first step towards creating and living a truly extraordinary life. *Ramsey Baby Steppers* use a very simple, straightforward 7-step plan that has worked for millions of everyday people just like you, regardless of income, education or net worth.

If getting your financial house in order is your top priority, what might be the second? It's called intentional living; i.e. living your life on purpose. If you don't know where you want to go or what you really want out of life, how can you possibly create, fund and live the life of your dreams? You can't. That's called leaving your life to chance, taking a gamble, which is the route that most people take and why most people live a mediocre, unfulfilled life.

There are only four steps required to live your life on purpose. (1) know exactly what you want, (2) have a strategic plan in place to get you from where you are to where you want to be, (3) a way to keep yourself held accountable and (4) track your results.

US Ambassadors For Prosperity was created to provide everyday people a general framework to as a guide to keep us on track in each of our areas of life. Our vision and mission is not just about money and building wealth; it is our deep desire to life a well-balanced life, to use our God-given gifts, talents, time and treasures to live lives that will make our communities, region, nation and world a better place to live, work and play. Our framework can be found in the back of this book.

Book 1 will be focused more on showing you what's possible and inspiring you to get your financial house in order. If you are reading this as an eBook, you may share your digital book with others. Be sure to leave a review on Amazon once you've completed the book. This helps us move up in the google ranking system.

You've heard it said that birds of a feather flock together. If you truly want to soar with the eagles don't hang out with the turkeys. Your income, net worth and quality of life or lack thereof is the average of the ten people in which you spend the most time. Are you living beneath your potential? If you're honest, you will say yes. If you're not inspired by the people around you on a daily basis, it's time to meet some new people!

US Ambassadors For Prosperity: We are ordinary people striving to live extraordinary lives. I invite you to join us on our exciting journey as we strive daily towards our mission: To create, fund and live a well-balanced life filled with purpose, achievement and financial prosperity; *a life worth smiling and talking about!*

Introducing…US Ambassadors For Prosperity!

I've found that life is much sweeter, way easier and much more productive when you have a tribe that shares a common vision, goals and objectives; i.e. everyone is heading in the same direction. When it comes to your making radical changes in your life, finding a supportive tribe is even more critical.

If you want to increase the odds and tip the scale in your favor, you must surround yourself with like-minded people with great attitudes. You need a support group that will be there in good times and bad; people who won't be afraid to tell you the truth, tell you what you need to hear and not what you want to hear, even when it hurts. People who will hold you accountable for results and won't accept mediocrity, excuses and less than the very best from your efforts.

There are 126 million households in America. 95% of Americans are heading in the wrong direction. Realize up front that you will be heading upstream against the current and will face resistance and obstacles. It will be tough at times, but you must never give up. When "life" happens and knocks you down, as it sometimes will…just get back up, dust yourself off and stick to the plan. Remember the vision you have for your life, don't look back, keep the focus on your future, not your past.

Attending a class, seminar or reading a book or two is not enough for most people to make and sustain a radical change in their lives. We get bogged down in the daily grind and if we aren't careful, we will fall back to our old habits of mediocrity, living unfulfilled lives. Don't let this be you!

We believe there is enough resources in this world to support all our endeavors and that God has given each of us a purpose to be on this planet. We want to help encourage and equip your passion and purpose! We provide a nurturing mastermind environment where our Members are encouraged to freely share and discuss their big bodacious dreams without fear or ridicule. A place to seek and give advice, share resources and invest in one another for the common good of the group.

You will be respected and valued as a human being and held to a standard to become the best possible version of you possible. Not as compared to your family, friends, neighbors and colleagues; as compared to the person you were yesterday and the day before. There is a big difference. You will be recognized and celebrated for your milestone achievements in every area of your life, no matter how large or small.

Join us online and offline in communities across America to share your journey. Your dreams, aspirations, daily trials, wins, celebrations, laughter and tear experiences are very important. It will provide the fuel and inspiration you need when you are feeling low. The daily wins prove that it is indeed possible for everyday people, not just a select few, to live extraordinary lives. It doesn't have to take a lifetime

to do it, just a strong will, support system and a plan.
May our experiences provide enough inspiration, hope, encouragement, and laughter needed to light a spark that can transform America, one community, one family at a time.

Perpetual Grant Fund: Proceeds from this book will be used to promote and fund a perpetual grant program for Ramsey Financial Coaches and Financial Peace University (FPU) Class Scholarships in communities across America.

Affordable Sponsorship and advertising options are available in the back of each publication for individuals, businesses and entrepreneurs beginning at only $25 each. Details can be found in the back of this book.

Donations of any amount are greatly appreciated. For a donation of $20, you are entitled to a free autographed paperback version of this book.

Royalty Rewards Program: There are 126 million households in America and 375 thousand in Northwest Florida. Help me spread the word and promote this program nationwide by joining our quarterly crowdfunding campaign. As my way of staying thank you, every time we receive a new or renewal registration, you will be eligible to receive a revenue-sharing royalty reward, month after month, year after year. Rewards will be split equitably among Supporters and Sponsors on a monthly basis based on new and renewal registrations received the month prior.

May God continue to abundantly bless each of you in the upcoming year!

Kindest Regards,
Nancy Gaskins – US Ambassadors For Prosperity
Jeremiah 29:11

ACKNOWLEDGMENTS

First and foremost, I must thank Dave Ramsey, the Baby Stepper Community and Ramsey Solutions. Dave took what most people would see as a huge financial failure and turned into an easy to understand and implement program that everyday people world-wide can use to get ahead financially.

He built a social media platform where Baby Steppers can gather, share stories and encourage one another daily.

His products and services are available to the masses at an affordable price. His continues to add value to his employees, clients and followers and is a man of quick wit, honesty, integrity, faith and generosity and encourages others to follow suit. People love working for and with him.

I admire the fact that he has built an empire from the ground up by helping others achieve financial success based on good ole fashion Biblical principles. He is a servant leader, has surrounded himself with team players who also have a heart for serving others. Entre-leadership is a fairly new term coined for Dave's ability to combine leadership with entrepreneurship. His methods are revolutionizing small businesses worldwide

To all my friends, family members, clients and followers: Thank you for believing in me and supporting me in my efforts to make our nation a better place to live, work and play by beginning first with helping everyday families build a rock solid financial foundation. I am eternally grateful.

For the non-Supporters, naysayers, pessimists and haters within my sphere of influence. Thank you for the fuel and inspiration that keeps me and everyone else moving forward. Every morning I get up with gratitude, look in the mirror, smile and straighten my crown because I know I'm who God says I am; I'm a winner and a child of the most high God!

1 INTRODUCTION

*Live like no one else, so one day you can
live and give like no one else.* ~ Dave Ramsey

Are you sick and tired of being sick and tired when it comes to your personal finances? Looking for a simple path with a proven track record filled with millions of success stories? If so, this book is for you.

The American Dream is alive and well for everyday people just like you and me, millions of people are proving it every day, so why aren't we hearing about it on the news?

Credit Suisse's "*Global Wealth in 2019*" measured the number of adult millionaires in the world. According to the report, the US has 18.6 million millionaires, the highest in the world.

DQYDJ.com had the following stats listed to show how your household stacks up against the top 10% in America. The threshold to be in the top 5% of household incomes in 2019 in the United States was $248,304.00.

What is the top one percent household income in the US in 2019? To be top 1% in the United States in 2019, you had to earn $475,116.00 or more as a household between January and December 2018.

That's the good news. The bad news is just because you might have a high-income bracket doesn't necessarily mean that you have a high net worth. In other words, you could be living paycheck to paycheck at a higher level of stupidity.

Inside these pages you will be introduced to the *Dave Ramsey Baby Steppers*. We are everyday people and our household incomes vary widely, which means we have different size shovels in which we use to achieve our goal of financial independence. We follow a very simple 7-Step financial plan formula that keeps us on track to achieve financial freedom. This method works for all of us no matter how big or how small our shovel.

In this book series you will learn who we are, what we do, how and why we do it. When it comes to money, Ramsey Baby Steppers have chosen to swim against the current trend followed by ninety-five percent of the population.

Follow the masses and you will end up just like them, broke and miserable, living paycheck to paycheck, up to your eyeballs in debt and a life filled with strife and stuff-itus.

Follow the Ramsey Baby Steppers and put yourself on a proven path that can change the financial trajectory of your life for generations to come. Join us to create, fund and life a life worth smiling and talking about!

We choose to "*live like no one else, so one day we will be able to live and give like no one else,*" a phrase coined by our Financial Mentor Dave Ramsey.

You can choose to continue to live a life of barely getting by, ho-hum mediocrity or decide today to join us to get on the fast track and make a difference with your life. It's not just about money, it's a new way of life, ideology and a generational legacy that Dave calls Financial Peace.

Most Americans look wildly successful because they have the house, cars, toys, clothes and lots of "stuff." Don't be fooled. The reality is they have lots of "debt," and no wealth. Keeping up with the Jones family, living paycheck to paycheck, neck deep in debt is robbing families of their ability to truly live the life of their dreams.

Money issues cause problems in the workplace, are a root cause of divorce and stress related illnesses. This doesn't have to be your story any longer. You can start a new chapter today, beginning with one little "baby step."

Millions of people that have followed the "Baby Steps" formula have had great success and so can you. Each year, thousands of FPU Classes are being conducted online and offline in communities across America.

Baby Steppers can be found in every age bracket, career field and income level. They are making a difference with their lives. They are transforming the communities in which they live. They are making their communities a better place to live, work and play. They live and give like no one else. You could be the next Baby Stepper success story.

I am a self-professed Dave Ramsey Baby Stepper. Don't worry if you don't know who or what that is because I will be explaining that over the next few pages. What is most important is that me and millions of other families know first-hand that Dave's program works. It's working for us so I know it will work for you.

In case you are wondering, I am not an affiliate or an employee of Ramsey Solutions. *I'm not getting paid to promote him or his services.* I believe in his methods and I respect him for who he is and what he stands for, which is why I personally use and highly recommend all his products and services.

We have 126 million households in America. Ninety-five percent are headed in the wrong direction financially speaking. Some aren't even aware of it because they are following the crowd, which seems like the "normal" thing to do.

Senior Citizens are not able to leave the workforce or are having to re-enter because they can't pay for their food, housing and healthcare. Student loan debt is crushing families. We have an unprecedented amount of people on government assistance programs. Most of these issues could be eliminated with the help of more financial education, coaching and accountability.

I have a dream in my heart to build a perpetual grant fund to train Financial Coaches and make them available as a resource to communities across America. Everyday people who have a servant's heart and are interested in becoming a financial coach for their community can apply for a financial grant. Recipients would be required to pay it forward by making a donation to replenish the grant fund, as well as provide a specified number of free coaching sessions as part of their commitment to community service.

As of this writing, the current price of the coaching program is listed at $1,795. Coaches that opt to join US Ambassadors For Prosperity Coaching team could earn $20 to $50 per hour based on their level of expertise, community service hours and client satisfaction scores.

The grant fund would also be used to provide Financial Peace University (FPU) classes and training resources to those who can't yet afford to participate. The current price listed for this 9-session class is $130.

Over 5 million families have already used this program to help them improve their personal finances, so it has a major track record for success. FPU Recipients would also be required to "pay it forward," by making a donation to our campaign that would keep the program funded into perpetuity.

Royalties received from the sale of this book and the other options listed below will help me fund this dream.

Earn As You Learn Investment Club Option: In addition to book royalties, the Program will be funded via a quarterly crowdfunded campaign.

Every 90-days, registered Sponsors and Supporter will contribute $30, $50 or $100 to the campaign. Campaign funds will be used to purchase residential real estate. The monthly rental income generated will be used to promote and fund the program into perpetuity, which means we will only have the fund the program *one time* and it will fund itself from that point thereafter.

Revenue-Sharing Royalty Rewards: As a thank you for your support, every time we receive a new or renewal registration, a percentage is set aside, designated as a *royalty reward* and distributed equitably among Supporters and Sponsors each month. Target Market Size:

126 million households. To become a registered Supporter or Sponsor, the campaign form is in the back of this book.

IN PURSUIT OF THE AMERICAN DREAM

Diary of a Baby Stepper

You guys! I could cry and I have to say, I have! Today I went to the bank to see if my last college loan payment had gone through, and it did! As of today, we are debt free!!

A little about my story. 5 years ago, I found myself going through a divorce with 3 lil ones (ages 18 months, 3, and 5 at that time). In Oct 2015, I ended up having to have an appendectomy and was hospitalized for 2 nights. Never in my mind would I had imagined that I would end up with a $32k medical bill. I had no help (because my credit was too good), no insurance, and what made it worse unable to work for 4 weeks without PTO.

During this time off, I learned I had been paying $10K interest on student loans 3 years in a roll and that after divorce I was left with $210K in debt. ($110k student loans, $24k land, $20k vehicles, $15k personal loan, $10k credit cards, and now about $32k in medical debt.)

I was physically, emotionally, and spiritually sick. I contemplated bankruptcy, but my pride wouldn't let me. I ended up selling my property and buying a mobile home as a temporary housing set up because I knew I could pay it off quick.

From Dec 2015-Dec 2018, I had worked my butt off and paid off $136k on my own (making anywhere from $60k-$90k). In Dec 2018, I married an amazing man who introduced me to Dave.

This year we paid off my remaining $74k together! I have been so blessed this yr. I thank my parents for watching my kids so many days and evenings so that I could take on extra work hours, my husband for supporting me, Dave for teaching me and my God for guiding me.

This journey is hard my friends, but you can do it! I wish each and every one of you a very blessed Christmas and new year to come! Keep digging!

Heather

2 IT'S OK TO BE WEIRD

Act your wage. Normal is broke. ~ Dave Ramsey

Most Americans look wildly successful because they have the house, cars, toys, clothes and lots of "stuff," but the reality is they have lots of "debt," and no net worth. In Texas they explain it this way, "*big hat, no cattle.*" Most everything they have on credit is either a depreciating asset or is no asset at all.

How wealthy are you? If you lost your income today, how long could you pay your bills with the cash you have available? Don't count credit cards. For example, if you have $10,000 cash in the bank and it cost you $2,500 per month to pay your bills, you have four months of wealth.

What's your net worth? Take the current market value of everything you own and subtract the amount you owe to any creditor. The remainder is your net worth.

Keeping up with the Jones family, living paycheck to paycheck, neck deep in debt is robbing families of their ability to truly live the life of their dreams. Money issues cause problems in the workplace, are a root cause of divorce and stress related illnesses.

Where you are today doesn't have to be how your story ends. You can start a new chapter today, beginning with one little "baby step." There's a better way to live.

"Live like no one else, so that one day, you can live like no one else." This is a mantra coined by the famous syndicated radio talk show host, New York Times Bestseller Author, Entrepreneur and personal finance expert Dave Ramsey. Millions of people follow his "Baby Steps" formula as a pathway to achieve financial independence and have had great success and so can you.

Unlike other personal finance gurus, Dave has walked the walk and talks the talk from the perspective of a man who has been in your shoes. He made it big, made mistakes, hit rock bottom and swore he'd never be in that financial position again. He made it out of the financial mess and now lives a life in which we all should aspire to attain.

Through his radio talk show, books, resources, subject matter experts at Ramsey Solutions and Financial Peace University network, he is able to reach and teach millions of people worldwide the very strategies that allowed him to pick himself up, get back up and stay up.

Inside these pages you will find stories from real people who are following Dave's advice and used his winning baby step formula to get ahead financially.

It's not an easy road to go against what everyone else is doing. Dave reminds us, *"it's okay to be weird."* Keep in mind, since ninety-five percent of all Americans are heading in the wrong direction, chances are…most everyone you know are going the wrong way and YOU just might be the only one swimming upstream. On the outside, you will look like you are the one with the problem. All your friends, family and co-workers will think you've gone off the deep end and lost your mind.

Once you make a commitment to get your finances in order, you must be prepared for what lies ahead and learn how to navigate around and overcome the obstacles that will stand in your way of achieving your desired financial result, which is financial freedom.

Some of these will be mistakes you make along the way. You will have to learn how to forgive yourself quickly, get back up and start over again. Some obstacles will be created by those you love. Good ole "Murphy" shows up for all of us, no matter if you have millions in the bank or are broke. But I can tell you one thing; it's a whole lot easier and less stressful to deal with Murphy when Baby Step 1 is completed!

I have listed some things below that you can expect to hear from friends and family. When you hear them or statements like them, your radar should go up immediately. These statements have been created by faulty thinking. Be careful of whom you take financial advice. Looks can be deceiving. Paycheck to paycheck can occur at any income level, education status or job title. No one is immune. These are programmed statements that we have bought into over the years from the people who want to keep us enslaved in debt!

Here's some examples: "It isn't possible to live without credit cards. You must have them to conduct business. I pay mine off every month and I get points and rewards for using it. How else could I pay for online shopping, Christmas and Vacations without a credit card? A car payment is just a fact of life, you will always have a car payment if you want to drive something nice. You can't get a college education without incurring tons of student loan debt. It's impossible to pay a mortgage off these days. The list just goes on and on.

All these stories of courage, setbacks, heartaches, encouragement, inspiration, small and large triumphs can be used as fuel to help lead you towards creating, funding and living a well-balanced life filled with purpose, achievement and financial prosperity; a life worth smiling and talking about!

IN PURSUIT OF THE AMERICAN DREAM

3 DAVE'S BABY STEPS

A budget is telling your money where to go instead of wondering where it went.
~Dave Ramsey

I am not an affiliate and I do not receive any type of compensation for promoting Dave, his business or his products. I'm just a happy customer who believes in his message, his products and services enough that I promote them and use them with my own Clients, friends, family and followers. No sense in reinventing the wheel when you have a winning formula for financial success for everyday people. Dave's Baby Steps provide both the foundation and framework for anyone at any age, income level or net worth status.

This is not a book designed to regurgitate Dave's teachings and philosophies. You can visit his website, listen to his podcasts and youtube channel, attend any of his events or purchase his products and hear it from the master himself.

However, since this book is a tribute to the Ramsey Babysteppers and I do recommend you follow his methodologies in regards to your personal finances, I would be remiss to not give you a little background and list the Baby Steps in this chapter for those of you who may not be familiar with Dave Ramsey or his work.

First and foremost, Dave has a mega track record for success. He has a background in finance and real estate, so naturally, he's a numbers guy and tracks everything. His Financial Peace University Classes are taught in thousands of locations across the nation. He has had over 5 million students go through the Financial Peace University program. On his website he lists all the stats on what you can expect based on the millions that have gone before you. That is powerful evidence of just how good the program is and how well it has worked for others.

His online Master Financial Coach Program is an online, interactive training program that has really gained traction over the past few years. The program was created using the data from the millions of people who have went through his program. In other words, he knows what your problems are, what obstacles you are most likely to encounter and how to help you solve them. There's probably not a financial issue that can't be addressed.

To learn more about his company, Ramsey Solutions, to order his products and services, to locate a Financial Peace University class, find a Financial Coach or other expert advisor, visit www.DaveRamsey.com. There is a plethora of free tools and invaluable information on his website.

I also highly encourage you to tune in and subscribe to his free podcasts and radio show live or on demand. One of the many cool things he does is allow people to call in or drop by the studio in Nashville to do their debt-free screams.

He hosts the *"Millionaire Hour,"* where real live millionaires call in and they share how they've achieved millionaire status.

The first book I recommend you start with is the *"Total Money Makeover."* Try your local library or you can buy it online at any book retailer or on Dave's website store. This book goes over each step, in complete detail, which gives you the framework from which you will be operating.

The baby steps are simple and easy to understand and will work for anyone no matter their income level. Many high income earners may think they are above it and dismiss the order in which they are listed, but there is a method to his madness and as you will soon find out from other Baby Steppers...stick with the plan, in the order in which he has it listed. It will prevent a lot of headaches and financial heartburn. Don't think too much and just follow the recipe. It works without fail. Every single time.

Some of you will follow some of the advice and not all of it; we call that being "Dave-ish." It's okay, just remember what happens when you mess with a proven recipe…could be a recipe for disaster or could just delay your results. Either way, it won't be the end of the world.

If you fall down, mess up and make a mistake, just get right back up and start again. Remember, "Murphy" happens to all of us. Life happens. Sometimes it may feel like Murphy has his own room at your house. The good news is that once you've started your baby steps, you will be in a better position financially when he does come knocking, so you can send him on his merry way!

Winning at money is 80 percent behavior and 20 percent head knowledge. What to do isn't the problem; doing it is. Most of us know what to do, but we just don't do it. If I can control the guy in the mirror, I can be skinny and rich.
~Dave Ramsey

Dave's Baby Step Formula

1. Save $1,000 Emergency Fund
2. Pay off debt using debt snowball
3. 3-6 month emergency fund
4. Invest
5. College Fund
6. Pay off house
7. Give

4 SIDE HUSTLES & DAVE CARS

Change is painful. Few people have the courage to seek out change. Most people won't change until the pain of where they are exceeds the pain of change.
~Dave Ramsey

Side Hustles and Dave Cars are always a hot topic of discussion among Baby Steppers.

I made one side hustle inquiry post in the Baby Steps Community Forum to see how much interest there was on me compiling a list and within 24 hours I had almost a thousand inquiries.

The post continues to draw interest and other posts ask the same question repeatedly. I plan on dedicating one book entirely to Side Hustles.

What Is a Side Hustle?
A side hustle is a side job or side gig. An additional job that a person takes in addition to their primary job in order to supplement their income.

Baby Steppers use a side hustle to help them increase their income so they can build their emergency fund, get out of debt faster and start building wealth.

I've included a list of <u>101 Side Hustle Ideas</u> in the back of the book. I'm sure you can find one that will spark your interest and can put some extra bucks in your pocket each week.

One of the first things Dave tells his followers to do is this: "Sell everything that isn't tied down. Sell so much stuff that the kids think they are next!" He says this tongue in cheek of course, but you get the point. Our closets, garages, kids rooms, attics and storage units are filled to capacity, bursting at the seams.

Most will admit that we have too much junk just sitting around collecting dust, not doing us any good. Sell it and you can buy it back later when you are in a better position financially. Chances are very high that you won't even miss the stuff when it's gone. Many Baby Steppers report feeling like a weight has been lifted off their shoulders when they declutter and reorganize.

It's Only Temporary

Most of us start out saying that our side hustle is only temporary. Others find out they enjoy the work or the extra cash so much that they keep doing it or they see an opportunity for the gig to replace their day job someday in the future.

There are exceptions, but Side Hustles typically aren't glamorous. They are a way to make some quick, easy cash, legally, of course. For many people, at first glance, you might find it beneath you to even consider taking a job as a pizza delivery guy or gal or something similar for fast cash. Again, I say, get over yourself and remember your goal, *"live like no one else, so one day, you can live like no one else."* You can do anything for a short period of time if you have a good enough reason.

This reminds me of a time in my life back in 2009. My spouse is a retired Army Veteran with a purple heart and bronze star. His career was unexpectedly cut short due to getting injured during the War in Iraq and we had to make some quick decisions on how our next Chapters were going to unfold.

Our finances were in limbo as we wouldn't know the outcome of his retirement and disability pay until two years later. That's a very scary place to be. We had a guarantee of an income source, but the range was so crazy that we couldn't begin to plan for our future.

We had dreamed of retiring to the Emerald Coast of Northwest Florida; the 100-mile stretch of sugar white sand and emerald green water located between Gulf Shore, Alabama extending to Panama City Beach, Florida. The problem was we were several years ahead of schedule timewise, but behind schedule financially. Not a good place to be.

Not one to have my dreams thwarted, I was sitting at my desk contemplating my situation. Out of the clear blue sky, I prefer to call it a divine intervention, I had remembered that I had done an internship for the Dollar General Corporation back years ago when I was in Grad School at Troy University. I didn't love it. I didn't hate it, but I can tell that you a career in retail was the farthest thing from my mind, but they did have locations all over the map and chances were very good that someone with my level of education and experience would be a prize catch. I was right.

I made a couple of phone calls and in less than an hour I had secured a Manager slot at a beach store in Destin, Florida with a good shot as District Manager. Small problem…I had a start date three days from now and nowhere to live.

My family and friends, which included my husband thought I had lost my mind. With my education, experience and pedigree, they attempted to shame me every time it was brought up. My hubby was embarrassed and wouldn't tell anyone where I was working! He soon got over it thought…especially when he was able to start reaping some of those benefits of sitting in the water with toes in the sand.

Over the years I had developed a knack for turning businesses around. I could go in and fix what was wrong, increase bottom line results, make a ton of money based on my results rather than hours worked and be on my way to the next gig.

What they didn't know was I had negotiated a nice salary package, filled with bonuses and incentives. Waivers had to be put in and approved, but because of all my education and experience, they made an exception and paid me well for my efforts. I brought that store up to the top three in the region and they stayed there on a consistent basis.

The Bottom Line?

You can do absolutely anything if you have a big enough WHY. I didn't care what kind of job I had to take if it meant I could go ahead and move to my dream destination. My dream was at stake. I would have taken less pay. I would have scrubbed toilets and mopped floors if that meant that I could move to Destin, Florida!

I kept myself motivated by remembering my "WHY." It was very easy decision for me to make and I didn't even have to call a friend or consult my husband. My choice was clear: I chose to move to paradise and I'd figure it all out as I went along!

Who Wants To Be An Entrepreneur?

Did you know that 48% of Americans dream of owning their own business? 51% are over 50 years of age and 69% start their businesses from home. The average startup is $10,000.

Do you have a dream in your heart to own and operate your own business? Starting your business as a Side Gig while you still have your day job might be the perfect time to spread your wings and give it a shot.

Do you have a great idea for a business and would like to turn that idea into cash? One of my areas of expertise is teaching people how to pitch and fund business ideas for profit and for fun. I also have an investment club for startups that provide grants for startups. Every time one of our sponsored projects generates a dollar, the project pays a revenue sharing royalty reward back to the grant fund. These rewards are then split equitably among the Supporter and Sponsors.

Not Everyone Wants To Be an Entrepreneur
Some of you may have a hobby, special interest or area of expertise that you could easily turn into a cash machine.
I have included some of the most popular side gig ideas that have been submitted to me by Baby Steppers and others who have chosen this route to get ahead financially.

Send Me Your Ideas & Links
Feel free to send me your ideas, pictures and links and I will include them in an upcoming edition.

DAVE CARS
What You Should Know

What Is a DAVE Car?
Although it irritates "Papa Dave," you will find that Baby Steppers use the term interchangeably to mean two very different things.

A Dave Car can be a *"get out of debt"* vehicle and is like a badge of honor for Baby Steppers. Used in this scenario, it describes a Baby Stepper's hooptie or beater car; the vehicle they buy with cash so they can move along the baby step and get out of debt faster. The basic premise is that you find a mechanically sound, reliable vehicle that you can pay for in cold hard cash. As long as it will get you from point A to point B without costing you an arm and a leg, it's a winner. Some of the pictures, stickers on the back of their cars and sales ads are hilarious.

A *"Dave Car,"* as defined by Dave himself is that dream car you've always wanted that you purchase with cash once you've completed the Baby Steps and can afford it.

Dave's Rule of Thumb When It Comes To Vehicles:
All of your vehicles and toys; i.e. cars, trucks, jet skis, motorcycles, or anything with a motor in it, should not total more than half of your annual income.

Why?
Because all of those things go down in value (depreciate) and as a percentage, you don't want half of your income tied up in things that are dropping like a rock.

When Can I Buy a New Car?
Dave doesn't recommend buying a new car until your net worth is more than $1 million. Ouch. I bet that got everyone's attention. You can learn "why" by listening in on some of his radio show calls where he explains his reasons.

Bottom Line:
Yes, Dave wants you to have a nice stuff, buy a new car and have

cool toys…but only when you can afford it!

If you are making $50,000 a year and you are driving a $50,000 truck…something is wrong with this picture. No, we are sorry, you don't "deserve it," because you work hard forty hours a week. Remember the *"big hat, no cattle,"* saying in Texas? That's you, so get over yourself!

Credit Karma reports the average monthly car payment in the USA was $554 for new vehicles and $391 for used ones originated in the first quarter of 2019.

That's a ton of money being spent on a depreciating asset that does nothing but go down in value. Baby Steppers have a better way, it's called the "Dave Car" Program.

Don't Quit On Me Now
I know most of you are shaking your heads right now in disbelief because you've been preprogrammed by 99.9% of Americans to believe that having a car payment is just a fact of life. Trust me when I tell you that it's just not true. Pride is what will keep most people from taking this seriously. All your friends, family members and colleagues drive nice, expensive vehicles. What would everyone say if you got rid of your nice ride and opted for something a little more…bleh?

Don't forget, those vehicles come with a nice fat payment book. Every time you get paid, note what percentage is going out on car and toy payments? Imagine how fast you could get out of debt if you took that same monthly payment amount and applied it towards your debt snowball or invested in some mutual funds.

If you stay committed and work the _Dave Car Plan_, you can get yourself back into a nice ride in a reasonable amount of time, but with zero payments.

How Does The Dave Car Plan Work?
Use a line item in our budget to set aside a few dollars each month so that in twelve to twenty-four months or whatever time frame you

choose, you can trade UP.

You can sell your current Dave car for cash, add the extra cash that you've saved with the sales proceeds and buy another, better quality "Dave Car."

After you have done this a few times, do the math and you will see that you can successfully trade yourself up to a nice ride, completely debt free!

Save All Your Buts…
We've heard all your excuses. We've made them ourselves. As long as your maintenance expenses each month are below what you would have spent on a car payment, you are winning. An added bonus is that chances are, you will more than likely not experience as much devaluation from your Dave Car! Many have driven their Dave Car hundreds of thousands of miles and got the amount they paid for back out of it when they sold it! That's a score!

I'm going to include a few pages of what current Baby Steppers have stated they are using as their "Dave Cars." It should give you some insight into what the most popular and most reliable makes and models.

What I found interesting was one of the top regrets that Baby Steppers have admitted as to being the dumbest thing they have ever done with money revolves around what? VEHICLES. Buyer beware. This is a real sore spot for many people and an area in which people lose a ton of money and experience a lot of heartburn and heartache. Listen to what people are saying and pay attention.

IN PURSUIT OF THE AMERICAN DREAM

Diaries of Ramsey Baby Steppers...
What's Everyone's Dave Cars?

- This is Larry my "Dave car" a 2006 Honda accord with 160k in miles. I've had Larry for 10 years lol we go way back.
- I bought this 2012 Honda a year ago, for my wife. It only had 17k miles on it when we bought it, now has 35k. It may seem like a pretty nice car, for a "Dave car", however we had a 2016 4Runner before this, that got 15-16 mpg, and had a huge loan balance and payment. This made a huge difference in our burn.
- We have an 05 Magnum. I got it for $1000. We were super broke, and it is our only vehicle. But second baby is on the way and we'd like to get a Toyota Sienna. Not a brand new one though, but one that is still in great condition.
- There's a common misconception on what a "Dave car" is... a lot of people assume it's the "beater" you drive while you're going through the baby steps when in reality it's the nice car you pay for with cash when you're done with the baby steps.
- Rather than get rid of my beloved car I moved lol. My Jeep Wrangler gets 22mpg, and before I moved, I was spending $60 a fill every week, sometimes twice. I moved to a more remote area closer to work and now I fill my car every 3+ weeks. And since I moved from one state to another my insurance also went way down. I figured those savings were enough to justify keeping my car since it's my dream car and I can budget and afford it while still saving... and I'm finally to the point that my car debt is my only debt
- We traded my husband's truck in for a an older Yukon xl Denali! Then we were in a car accident this summer that totaled it and we waited a little bit and then bought a Cadillac Escalade platinum for $30K insurance check paid for the most of this car and we paid cash for the rest). It's awesome! I never thought as a kid that I'd have awesome cars! Haha! Currently saving for our next car to replace our 2010 Ford Edge that has been paid off for years! Love not having car payments!
- That Honda will last you forever. I had a Honda for ten years. Great choice. Dependable and no issues except maintenance.
- I have a 2013 Honda crv and loveeeeee it! Only reason I would

get a different car is if I have another child I'll need space for another car seat!!! But it has been great for gas mileage, safety, practicality for my family, and have barely had any maintenance issues!! Great choice!

- Same!! We have a '13 CRV and I have no complaints. We are about to trade it in for an Odyssey since we will have three in car seats come May.
- Consider selling privately over "trade in" as you'll get better value from the sale!
- 15' Carolla is our Dave car 100,000 mi still going strong will keep it til the wheels fall off
- My Dave car would be a F350, but since my outlook on life has changed, it would probably be a nice small suv like this.
- Here's my Dave car. 2008 Ford Focus with 200k miles.
- 2007 Honda Odyssey with 117xxx miles. I LOVE it
- Nice! I miss my 2016 4 Runner too. Traded it in for a cheaper car. Saves a ton on gas and allows me to get out of debt quicker. One day when I am out of debt, I will pay cash for a 4Runner.
- Our 4Runner was my wife's "baby" she let it go clawing and kicking. Doesn't really like this Honda, because it doesn't "look" cool. But it is saving us a boat load of cash.
- I have a 2006 4runner with 170k....needs alternator...gonna fix it and sell it ...good for somebody Dave car.....hurts my heart to part with it
- Our "hooptie" 2007 Toyota sequoia. Bought it almost 2 years ago, after baby number 4 was born, & we LOVE it!!! It took a while to sell our car with the lien on it, but we paid it down, until we did, & were able to sell it for the balance on the loan!
- My husband's Dave car is a 3-year-old Toyota Tundra - so I will say it is a 2019 Toyota Tundra
- This is the Dave car we bought for my wife last year. 2019 Volvo XC40. We took delivery of it in Sweden through Volvo's Overseas Delivery program.
- We saved money buying a new car. Old car was getting maybe 10mpg. Costing us about $300-$400 per month in gas.
- 1999 F 350 with 400,000
- 2001 Suburban with 275,000

- 2005 Odyssey with 287,000
- While I think about "upgrading" my vehicles occasionally, I'm also blessed to be a stay at home mom of 6 kids plus take care of 3 extra children, all homeschooling, all living in my means of my budget easily.
- Sure, pretty things appeal to me but the peace of mind my lifestyle brings is everything right now.
- Goal currently is to buy a newer 15 passenger Transit. Patience is a virtue while we build cash
- 2004 Jeep Grand Cherokee
- 05 Nissan Xterra paid $2500 for it long before we ever even considered starting the Dave life. We have been very fortunate for how well it has been mechanically. Due to meds I was on it has a small dent in the back-quarter panel that I refuse to fix as a daily reminder to always research my medication. Medically retired this year so it should last way past us being out of debt.
- We just got rid of our 2012 money pit... I mean CR-V. They thought it was a lemon though.
- 2007 Pontiac Grand Prix
- This is my car!! I LOVE mine and planning on keeping it forever (I won't buy used because of a really terrible experience) so I buy cars that last......I've had mine for 7 years already.
- The one on the right is our Dave truck. It's mine. We were able to sell our 2007 Yukon XL for a few more grand (to the dealership!) than what we owed on it. We turned around and used the difference to help pay cash for the 2003 Tahoe with 160k miles on it. The best part is that the Yukon needed about $4k worth of work before we could drive it across country the following week with a camper hooked on to it, and this truck needed nothing! We came out so far on top, driving it just brings me joy.
- The Yukon is my husband's and should have been a Dave car but he financed it before he believed in Dave. We don't owe a ton on it but it'll be paid in full next year!
- First off I wish I drove that little. I had a 2017 4runner. Yes. Gas mileage was awful. Ended up surprise divorced and received it free and clear. Sold it for 33k in pocket. Bought a Honda crv

myself. I since swapped it out because I needed towing power. But Honda's are great vehicles.

- Honda, It's a tight squeeze and we can't all go anywhere together, but it's temporary, right? At least it's easy to drive and bop in and out of parking spaces!
- I have a hooptie! 2001 New Beetle. Paid $1,500
- Well what's in between a hooptie and "Dave car" It's not a Lamborghini, but not a hooptie either, paid cash. But we're not out of debt. I'm gonna keep calling it a "Dave" car. That's what my wife and I had to tell ourselves to get on the program, so such it will be.
- I moved to a walkable community, so my two feet get me from point A to B. Saved thousands of dollars by not owning a car anymore.
- This is my cheapo super beat up (got smacked by someone in the rear) Subaru Outback.
- My dream car? The new Subaru ascent or forester. I always wanna drive a subie.
- Great Dave car! We have a 2011 CRV and is still running great! We bought it new before following Dave, but the car is paid off and running in great condition. We love Honda's in our family!
- Nice car! I drive an 02 CRV now and it's a great car. It has been a little finicky with a couple things, but once I learned that, no issues
- I have a 2002 Lexus and I love it
- My Dave car - 2019 Lexus UX 250h
- 2014 Kia Forte paid cash, and it just got the engine replaced because of a recall before we bought it. I will add that it was only $7k and they offered a higher trade in value for our previous car with a loan because we said we only had $8500 for the new car and upside down. They were amazing! Won't buy a car from anyone else because of that experience.
- I bought a Toyota Corolla 2000 got the sticker on my car that says Dave's hooptie! I'm realizing it's not a David car-it's an actual hooptie but no car payment!

- 05 Acura MDX with 150K miles, third owner. Great car but starting to give us problems. We've started a car fund for the day the repair cost more than it's worth.
- Our Dave car... bought it two weeks ago. 2012 Toyota Camry SE 64k. My Highlander before 06 had 120k when we bought her 154k when we traded for the Camry lasted a year and a half and just wasn't worth fixing anymore.
- 2011 Ford Edge. Bought new, first new car since 1986. I'll drive it as long as the wheels will turn.
- My "Dave Car" would for sure be a tesla but my hoopties right now is a 2013 smart car and a 01 Ford explorer.
- 2003 Chevy Silverado 1500 Z71. 240k, runs like a top because I happily pay for maintenance as it comes up, purchased in 2013 for 10k on loan. Used it for my failed furniture business and now with a career change, I still side hustle furniture and appliances with it, will run this baby til the wheels fall off.
- 2010 Ford Crown Vic. Got rid of our 2007 Jetta and got this a year ago. Minimal repairs so far!!!!
- 2004 Buick LeSabre. Purchased it with 33k miles on it this past March after I got in an accident in my 1998 Ford Expedition last December. Otherwise I would probably still be driving it with 255k miles on it. It was a great car.
- 2003 Highlander 216k miles on it.
- 05 GMC Envoy for 2.5k cash about a year ago.
- 2005 Pontiac Grand Am. Around 200k miles on it. I've had it since before my husband and I got married 12 1/2 years ago (I got it in '06...my mom bought it for me). My husband uses it to commute to work. We also have a tiny 2017 Hyundai Accent with about 60k on it. We bought it 8 months ago. Traded hubby's fancy truck in for it. We still have a loan on it, but much more reasonable than the truck was.
- I have 2013 CR-V that I bought from my dad in 2014 and it has been paid off for 2 years! Hubby has a 2012 F150 that we paid cash for when we bought it. It is soooo nice having NO car payments!!

IN PURSUIT OF THE AMERICAN DREAM

- 2002 GMC Safari and a 2003 corolla
- 2012 Honda Civic LX sedan. 50,000 miles
- We have a 2006 Honda van and my husband's work vehicle is a 1996 Chevy suburban
- 2010 Honda Insight woth 150k miles
- If you bought it for cash, it's a Dave car! It doesn't have to be a broken-down piece of junk. My daughter's car is a beautiful 2004 Nissan Murano. Paid cash, 6200.00
- 04 Saturn Vue. 230000 miles on it. Still running and gets me from point A to B.
- 2012 Chrysler T&C.
- Needed a new (to us) family car and paid less than 10K.
- Had higher miles than why we originally wanted, but it came fully loaded (not expected) and was what we needed and more.
- We will have it paid off and own it before having it for a full year!
- 2011 Ford Escape. Sold my 2018 Toyota Highlander and therefore knocked out over $20,000 in our snowball. I love this little car!!!
- My "Dave" car is a 2002 Honda Civic with 118,000 one owner (me) miles. I see no need to replace it any time soon...and we're BS6.
- From a 2018 (bought in 2018) Honda Pilot EX-L with Honda Sensing, blacked out, fully loaded to this 2013 200k mile base model van but we're saving almost 600/month on payments...
- I have a 2005 Prius with almost 300,000, I love it!!

5 WHEN MURPHY COMES KNOCKING

Stupid is not illegal. ~ Dave Ramsey

Murphy's law is an adage that states, "Anything that can go wrong will go wrong."

Matthew 5:4 of the Holy Bible can be paraphrased, "the sun rises on the evil and on the good. The rain falls on the just and the unjust."

Life happens to all of us and no one is immune, including those with big, small or average size bank accounts.

The good news is that typically when Murphy comes knocking at your door, it is always at the most inopportune time; in between paydays, when you are broke or unemployed.

It usually puts the average person into a financial tailspin that takes them months if not years to overcome and get back to the starting point.

Psst…it's never a good time to hear Murphy's knock at your door but there are things that you can do to make it a lot less stressful and painful.

It Starts With Step ONE
In my opinion, Baby Step ONE is the most powerful and most important baby step of all. I guarantee you if I had of followed this

path I would not have experienced so much financial headache and heartache and distress over the years.

One thousand dollars is not a ton of money, but it can be a real lifesaver when you are broke. It also gives you a buffer and peace of mind, which is invaluable.

When the tire blows, the transmission goes out, your frig breaks down or you get sick and have to miss work and you don't have any personal time left, or a loved one passes away unexpectedly and you have to go out of state… trust me, that $1,000 is a game changer.

Murphy Incidents
I've included some examples of real incidents that Baby Steppers have experienced. Some are heartbreaking, some you would expect, some you won't believe, like the one I read today where a guy was driving to his mom's house and he hit a *catfish* and it busted his windshield.

You read that right. Evidently, a bird was flying overhead (must have been a large bird) and dropped a very large catfish it was holding in its talons and it hit his car! He posted a picture of the catfish. Hilarious, but true and it will cost him and his insurance company some money to fix his windshield. I hope he had his emergency fund in place!

Moral Of The Story:
Expect the unexpected and have your $1,000 emergency fund in place.

Send me your Emergency Fund stories to include in an upcoming edition. How did you raise the money and how long did it take?

6 WHERE WE INVEST

Compound interest is the 8th wonder of the world. ~Unknown

What Does Dave Say About Investing?
Dave's philosophy is to get out of debt, invest 15% of your income in tax-favored retirement accounts. Invest in good growth stock mutual funds.

He suggests that we hold four mutual funds in our 401(k) or IRA; one growth fund, one growth and income fund, one aggressive growth fund and one international fund.

An investor's worst enemy is often our self, which is why I value Dave's suggestions. His message is simple, easy to understand and straightforward. It requires patience and is not a get rich quick template.

We have all heard the 8th wonder of the world is compound interest and the sooner we start investing the better, but…yes, there is always a but.

If you follow the Baby Step formula and get our of debt first, you will have a lot more income to invest, which will make a larger impact on your financial future in the long run.

In 2019, Ramsey Solutions conducted the largest survey of millionaires ever with 10,000 participants. You might be surprised with the findings.

Bottom Line:
The millionaires did it through consistent investing, avoiding debt like the plague and smart spending. No lottery tickets. No inheritances. No six-figure incomes.

They worked, saved and invested an average of 28 years before hitting the million-dollar mark. Most of them hit the milestone at age 49.

National Study of Millionaires by Ramsey Solutions Results

- Eight out of ten millionaires invested in their company's 401(k) plan.
- Three out of four invested outside of company plans.
- The top five careers for millionaires include engineer, accountant, teacher, management and attorney
- 79% of millionaires did not receive any inheritance at all from their parents or other family members.

Recommended Resources:
For more details, I recommend you read Chris Hogan's newest book, Everyday Millionaires: *How Ordinary People Built Extraordinary Wealth and How you Can Too.*

This book is based on the National Study of Millionaires completed by Ramsey Solutions.

7 CASH FLOWING COLLEGE

College is expensive. Paying for it is one of the most challenging financial problems in America. Many parents sacrifice their future financial well-being and many students enslave their future earnings by taking out student loans to cover the cost.

I hate to admit that I am one that fell for *"Student Loan Stupidity"* to pay for my (MBA) Masters in Business Administration. I was working full-time and going to school full time and wanted to get it all knocked out in one year. The degree doubled my income, but I later got into a financial bind and that one mistake has cost me thousands of dollars and nothing but headache, heartache and regret. I'm still paying for that mistake. I do NOT recommend it.

Baby Steppers are cash flowing degrees and as I learn more, I will be sharing their tips and techniques in upcoming editions.

WHAT YOU SHOULD KNOW

According to the Federal Reserve:
- American owe over $1.6 trillion in student loan debt.
- The average student loan debt per graduate is $35,000
- Estimated 44 million student loan borrowers in America
- It can take anywhere from 10 to 30 years to repay student loans

Average Price Tags For Annual Tuition and Fees
- Public two-year college for in district students: $3,660

- Public four-year college for in-state students: $10,230
- Public four-year college – out of state students: $26,290
- Private four-year college: $35,830

Source: www.research.collegeboard.org

58% Graduation Rate
42% Did NOT Graduate

Bottom Line:
Four out of ten times a student loan recipient does not graduate and get a degree. Let that sink in for a minute.

Consolidation Loans For Student Loan Stupidity
The ONLY time that Dave suggests ever getting a consolidation loan is for student loans and he has a preferred provider that he recommends.

The reasoning is simple. He says you can't dig yourself out of a hole by digging a deeper hole. In other words, don't go into more debt to cover up your old debt.

Many people think if they had more income and it would solve all their problems. You've got to change your old habit and get rid of your old mindset of using debt to solve your problems. Managing your cash and living within your means is your issue. If you don't, you will still be living paycheck to paycheck, just at a higher level.

Recommended Resources:
Debt-free Degree by Anthony O'Neal.

Have you or someone you know cash flowed a college degree?

Send me details on how you did it and I will include it in a future edition.

8 MORTGAGE FREE

Your home is likely the biggest investment you'll make in your life, which can also make it your biggest risk. Buying your first home should be an exciting time – in a bust-out-the-champagne sort of way, not a bust-out-the-Xanax kind of way.
~L. Grossman

Back in the day of your grandparents or great grandparents for some of you, it was very commonplace and a high priority to become mortgage free. The ritual was usually a big family celebration that included lighting the mortgage on fire.

Today, it is quite the opposite. We are cash poor and house rich. Our homes make up the bulk of all our wealth. A home is typically the largest investment we will make in our lifetime.

With that said, I am continually shocked about how so many people are so clueless when it comes to buying a house. They go into debt for hundreds of thousands of dollars the same way they go into debt and buy a car…usually without much consideration. Carrying a 30-year mortgage for life is now considered "normal."

Mortgage Free Status is Possible
Baby Steppers may be considered abnormal, but we are achieving mortgage free status on a daily basis. It warms my heart to see the daily posts and pictures of families young and old who are choosing to live a life of financial freedom that includes being "mortgage free."

What Dave Says About Buying a House
You should be out of debt, equipped with an emergency fund of three to six months of expenses and have at least a 10% down payment. Twenty percent is even better and will keep you from paying private mortgage insurance on top of your monthly mortgage payments.

Dave recommends your housing payment, including property taxes and insurance, to be no more than 25% of your take-home income. To maximize your savings, you should get a 15-year, fixed rate mortgage.

Why?
Although a 15-year mortgage has higher monthly payments, the interest rate is lower and you will be paying off the principal faster, which means you'll pay a lot less in interest over the life of the loan. You will be in debt for half the time.

How Do You Get a Mortgage Without a Credit Score?
Note I didn't say "bad" credit score. If you are living a debt-free lifestyle, you will have a solid financial foundation and eventually your credit score will be ZERO…yes, you read that right.

Having "no score" to a Baby Stepper means you've more than likely mastered the art of living debt free and are now focused on building your net worth.

A credit score is a story that is told about how you manage your money. TransUnion, Equifax and Experian are credit bureaus that use credit-scoring models like FICO to come up with a score.

Yes, you can get a mortgage with a ZERO credit score. You will need to find a lender that does manual underwriting.

Manual underwriting is a hands-on investigation into your ability to repay debt. You will need 20% or more for a down payment, since it reduces the lenders risk.

You will have to submit documents that prove you're financially responsible. The more evidence you can provide, the higher your chances of qualifying for your mortgage.

Examples of documents you could use:
Income verification for the last 12-24 months and a steady payment history for at least four regular monthly expenses, such as rent, utilities, phone, cell phone or cable, insurance premiums, childcare or tuition.

Mortgage Free?
Every day Baby Steppers are posting their "mortgage free" statuses and pictures on our community pages. Feel free to share your story and picture and I will include it in an upcoming edition.

IN PURSUIT OF THE AMERICAN DREAM

9 GIVE LIKE NO ONE ELSE

Live like no one else, so that one day, you can live and give like no one else.
~Dave Ramsey

I long for the days where I am able to "GIVE" like no one else. I constantly seek out ideas where I can perform random acts of kindness and generosity towards others.

Baby Steppers are some of the most generous people on the planet when it comes to giving! You've probably heard the old saying, "it's better to give than to receive," but you won't know that feeling until you've been able to experience it first-hand.

It's a Small World
Just a few days ago, on my local community page someone posted a random act of kindness from a stranger. They had their restaurant tab picked up by someone and on the ticket were these words written in ink, "Merry Christmas! #Dave Ramsey, #Babystep 7, Generosity Generates Goodness."

I loved it so much that I posted it to our Ramsey Babystep Community group page and within 24 hours I had over 1,000 likes and posts and the number continues to grow as I am writing!

Our group page is comprised of people from all over the world and it was interesting to see LOCAL baby steppers in my region that I have not yet met, chime in on the post because they read the name of the restaurant on the ticket. What was most exciting, however, is the person that was responsible for the kind act of generosity saw the post and was able to see the impact her kind deed had on the recipient as well as the community at large. Priceless.

Thanksgiving is over and now we are just a few days before Christmas. Everyone is in the giving spirit. Social media and the news is filled with heartwarming stories of people doing kind things for one another, but what if…

What If…
You had the financial means to perform financial random acts of kindness (miracles) *all year long,* (not just during the holidays) every time you felt the nudge in your spirit telling you that you should "do something."

Some examples I've recently read:
- Local business owner pays 36 families' utility bills for Christmas
- Local church pays overdue school lunch tabs
- Son pays off single mom's mortgage
- Organization builds tiny homes for homeless Vets
- Man and wife gifts a car to someone in need

The Importance Of Tithing
A tithe is 10% of your income given specifically to your local church. While it's important to give your time and talents, the word tithing refers to giving money.

An offering is anything extra that you give beyond the tithe.

Tithing helps us keep our priorities straight. It is an act of faith and demonstrates that we trust God with our lives and our finances. The tithe is not for God's benefit, it is for ours. God doesn't need our money; he owns it all. We are only managers of what He's given us.

Leviticus 27:30
"A tenth of the produce of the land, whether grain or fruit is the Lord's, and is holy."

Proverbs 3:9
"Honor the Lord with your wealth, with the first fruits of all your crops."

2 Corinthians 9:7
"Each of you should give what you have decided in your heart to give, not reluctantly or under compulsion, for God loves a cheerful giver."

Bottom Line:
Tithing is about the heart. It is an important part of faith for those of us who follow God and your tithe should be money you set aside first, not last, which means it's a priority and not an afterthought.

Tithing means you're being obedient to God, so you should give without expecting anything in return.

With that said, you'd be hard pressed to find anyone who is a faithful tither that would say that they have not benefitted many times over than the value of their tithe.

You Reap What You Sow
I like to explain it using the analogy of a farmer and his crops. He plants a few seeds, does his part keeping his crop watered, fertilized, weeded and pest free and then turns it over to God. God rewards him with a bountiful harvest many times over the actual seeds he has sown.

When you tithe to God and are generous towards others who are less fortunate *and* you give with a servant's heart, you are planting seeds. Those seeds will germinate and produce a bountiful harvest for both the giver and the recipient; a life worth smiling and talking about!

Do You Have a "Random Act of Kindness" story and picture you'd like to share?
Send it to me and I will include it in an upcoming/revised edition.

IN PURSUIT OF THE AMERICAN DREAM

SHOWING GENEROSITY IS THE MOST FUN YOU CAN HAVE WITH MONEY
Diaries of Ramsey Baby Steppers

- Today I celebrate the ability to fulfill a childhood dream. Today I was able to present my mom with keys to her new house. My Mother worked for Remington's for over 30 years and raised three boys. She bought and paid for her home and property. I couldn't save the house, but I was able to remove the house and build a new one.
- By the worlds account my brothers and I should have been a statistic being raised by a single mother, but my mother was also a praying mother.
- I want to first thank my GOD LORD and SAVIOR for giving me the resources and planning my steps. Thanks to my two brothers _____. They worked themselves to the ground moving my mom out in time before the bulldozers moved in. This is definitely a blessing from GOD! I love you Mom!
- Kindness Ripple Effect: when you show kindness and patience some day you will be rewarded.
Although in babystep 2 my kids were hungry and I still had several more errands to run and our van AC stopped working- so I thought ok I will go get the kids a happy meal and use my miscellaneous money I usually save for Diet Coke for myself at work at night. I let the woman in the other lane go ahead of me- got to the register to pay and it was already covered by the woman in front of me. I so look forward to being pat baby step 3 and having he freedom to do things like this. Although I cannot bless someone with money I can bless them with patience and kindness. :) making the word a better place one smile and wave and a time.

Our family is currently on BS2 with about 7-8 months left. I am an elementary school nurse and our daughter is a first grader. Over the weekend, our school lost one of our sweet kindergarten girls (6 years old) in a tragic hiking accident. My sweet girl decided to donate $30 from her savings to the family of the little girl. She only gets $7 a week for allowance and chores so it took her 5 weeks to earn this amount of money.

She was so proud to give this to the principal this morning for the family. Proud mom moment & wanted to share with all the fellow Baby Steppers who are also trying to raise good, kindhearted, giving humans. We can't wait until Baby Step 7 so we can live and GIVE like no one else.

- Thank you all for your encouragement, kindness, advice and testimonies! You all truly blessed and uplifted my spirit today. I'm so blessed by your thoughts and prayers! With so many prayers warriors I know I can make it through this storm. I have contacted his psychiatrist to alert him of this behavior and relapse. My hope is that this doctor will help get him the support and treatment necessary. Again, thank you all for your help your continued prayers. I will read these posts often to stay encouraged. Blessings!
- Happy/kind of saddish moment today:
- I paid for the guy behind me at the drive-thru where I got my diet Coke and the cashier said he had worked there fourteen years and had NEVER had anyone pay for the person behind them. That made me sad - why would that be a foreign idea????
- Anyway, I loved the guy's reaction behind me when I saw the cashier shake his head "no", and point to me. I was so happy... It was only $5 but I think the guy was blessed.
- I'm on step 4 but trying to to step 7 as often as I can.
- Random Acts of Kindness: Today we were on the receiving end.
- The kids and I were eating dinner tonight at IHOP. I enjoy bonding with my kiddos over dinner when it's possible. It was my Daughter's idea today to go have her pancakes with sprinkles. ☐ As I was getting ready to ask for our ticket to pay, our waitress comes back to our table and said that our meals were paid by a person who walked in and felt generous to pay for everyone's meal in the restaurant!! ☐ (jaw drop). My kiddos were also blown away and thankful for this act of kindness. I loved my 14 year-old Son's reaction.. "When I follow Dave Ramsey's babysteps and I'm on BS7, I want to pay for people's meals just like this person did for us!" "Live Like No One Else So Later You Can Live and Give Like No One Else" -D.R.

LIFE OF A BABY STEPPER

Everyday Life
Dumb Stuff We've Done With Money
Debt Free Screams
When Murphy Comes Calling
101 Side Hustle Ideas

Contact me to include your story, experience & picture in an upcoming edition.

EVERYDAY LIFE

This was posted on my local community page. Baby Steppers, we are making a difference in our communities, one family at a time! Keep it up and keep being weird!

> Went to Cactus Flower on Monday night, the service was excellent, the food was hot and tasty and we had enough left over for lunch the next day. To top of a great meal, some wonderful person anonymously paid for our dinner! We were so surprised and very, very thankful. Truly brought tears to both our eyes. Merry Christmas everyone!!

A sense of humor is a must for all Baby Steppers!

The best way to save on a water bill!
Photo courtesy of C. Sanchez

I don't have anyone else I can share this with as I grew up in a family that wasn't great with money, so I thought I'd share it with people who understand. This is my last card to pay off for BS2. I have already paid off $6,000 since May of this year when my husband deployed. While he was away, I started working three Dave Jobs (teaching dance, mystery shopping, and private contract therapy) in addition to my full-time hospital job. In December alone, I put a little over $1,100 toward this card. Despite it all, I'm dang proud of myself for my hard work! ☐ I've made it a goal to have all credit cards paid off by July 2020. $4178.56 to go until I'm debt free. Gazelle intensity, right? (TB)

****

Needed new sneakers for going to the gym but didn't have the extra $40+ it would be for a decent pair. Happened to go into DSW to look around. Got handed a $15 gift card just for going in and my mom gave me hers too. Found a pair of Under Armor on clearance for $54.98. Went to the register, cashier gave me 25% off plus the sale price. Total after all discounts and gift cards came up to $2.99. Safe to say, I got them. (AC)

****

So I took FPU in April/May then paid off my new car, $41K, in 7 months! So last night I tipped the bill with a Merry Christmas to our server! Felt great! (KJ)

****

We are officially on to BS3. We got out of our fleeced car tonight. We had to pay to do it, but we did it. All cards and student loans paid off. On to building up our emergency fund. We bought a used car in cash and we are ready to ring in a new decade with ZERO debt!!! (K.M)

****

Today was a good day. With my final paycheck of 2019, WE PAID OFF THE LAST MY STUDENT LOANS!!! We still have my wife's loans to go, but since she's still in school we don't have any more monthly payments

This marks a halfway point in our debt-free journey, only 8 months in! I'm feel so blessed to say that in only 4 years since graduating with my bachelor's degree I earned a master's degree also and no more debt from the undergrad!!

The Lord is good. (E.L)

It's a beautiful day! I officially "own" my bachelor's and master's degrees free and clear!! No longer a slave to student loan debt!!! Sometimes God gives us a God-sized dream to have us step out in faith and push fear and our doubts aside. $9892 gone in three months and $73148 gone overall. Thank you, Jesus, and thank you Financial Peace University! (EB)

****

Yay! We tipped the bill tonight. We both knew the girl who was a awesome waitress. Felt great to tip the bill! Being a waitress, it is great to get a tip like this! Paying it forward. (SS)

****

I'm Debt Free! YAY! What a feeling!$15,000 in 364 days. I can't stop smiling. I did it! All by myself! Thanks, Dave Ramsey, for the encouragement! (JB)

****

We have a 3-year-old daughter who has had a ton of medical issues over the last two years including lots of pain and fevers. We just got a diagnosis but it's a rare genetic issue that we will have to travel from Texas to Cincinnati for care/treatment/guidance. We don't know how many trips will be needed or what her care will cost in the future, so we have no idea what to budget. We don't want to put everything on hold forever. This is especially stressful when we have so many bills looming already! Any ideas? We are already stockpiling money for it but we really would like to keep the snowball rolling! (TW)

Y'all, I can't believe this...as of 6:00pm tonight I made my very last student loan payment!!!!!

I took Financial Peace University in the fall of 2016 as a 29-year-old cynic. The class changed my life. At the time I had $62,000 in debt from student loans, and while I had no outstanding cc debt, so much of my money trickled away from me through the regular use of 10+ credit cards. It took me an additional year to stop being "ish", but once I did, I ended up gazelle-intense paying off the remaining $52,000 in two years on a yearly income of $49,000! This process has taught me so much about how I want to live my life, particularly as someone doing life on my own. I've learned so much about self-control, sacrifice, embracing being weird in the eyes of others, and the freedom of not having anxiety about my finances.

If you're here but still on the fence or suspicious about Ramsey, or just not a "joiner," I totally get it. That was me. But I'm telling you, it's not a cult thing - Dave is NOT some snake charming salesman selling miracle water, and we BS followers are not mindless automatons. Dave teaches a biblical financial mindset with daily practical steps for people who are focused and ready to embrace a counter-culture financial mindset. And I swear to you: this mindset can and will change your life. (AA)

****

Because I'm on the Dave Ramsey plan and only on baby step 2, I can't afford to spend money at a bar on this wonderful Friday night. So my wife and I made homemade "Old Fashions" ☐ at our Home Bar (kitchen counter). Stay the course and maintain the debt free journey. Debt is dumb, cash is king! **(TA)**

****

I've realized I have a Poverty and Victim Mentality. For those of you who have overcame this, how did you do it? What are good books to read? I don't desire to be like this any longer. Thank you in advance for your help. (VY)

****

Just listened to The Dave Ramsey Show from yesterday where he talked about how all the debt free screams from this year totaled 37 million dollars (if I remember correctly!) this year!! Just wanted to shout out all the people in this group are debt free/are making HUGE strides in becoming debt free! You are all such an inspiration to me & my husband on BS2!! Excited to continue being gazelle intense in 2020! (CA)

****

So today is good day in our baby steps!! We were able to get a Lemon case settlement and got all of our money back plus inconvenience money. One debt less in our snowball. All the money is going towards my truck, about $18k, this will bring it down to $6k left.. it feels good to be so close to be debt free. (OT)

****

What is everyone doing with their Christmas bonus? (KE)

****

I was in line at Walmart yesterday. As usual, they had 6 regular registers and 10+ self-checkouts closed and it was crazy slammed. I wandered around for a minute and finally picked a line. There was this sweet older woman in front of me. She put half of the stuff from her cart on the belt and asked the cashier to just ring up this stuff to start because she wasn't sure she would have enough for everything. Guys, she was just buying food. I told her to please put the rest of her stuff up and I would pay the difference. She tried to argue, but I told her to please just let me buy her groceries. That nobody should have to go without food.

****

I was nervous because we are in baby step 2 and running a zero budget, but I could just feel God telling me to trust him and do it. She put the rest up, paid what she could, and the remainder was $29.87. Guess how much I padded our Christmas budget line item for "just in case"? $30. When I saw the total, I had tears in my eyes. She gave me a hug and I told her Merry Christmas and that Jesus loves her.

******

I'm not sharing this to brag or look for kudos. I believe I did what most others in this situation would do. But I wanted to share about how trusting God with our finances and listening to him and taking these opportunities to show others His love always works out. (JM)

IN PURSUIT OF THE AMERICAN DREAM

I've noticed lots of folks posting about feeling conflicted about giving back while on BS2 so I thought I'd share my story:

A co-worker of mine was feeling broken up about only being able to afford one Christmas gift for her daughter. Before really thinking, I found myself volunteering to get her a few gifts from Santa. When it set in, I panicked a bit about being on BS2 and volunteering to do that. Welp, I followed through and spent about $50 from my gift budget and figured I'd make adjustments for my other holiday spending.

Today my husband's Grandparents sent us $100 in our Christmas card! They're very generous people and usually send us some yummy goodies for the holidays, but we never count on them sending cash. It's just funny how things work out sometimes.

Hope this helps if you've been feeling conflicted about giving back this holiday season! If you have the ability to give or can make some adjustments to do so—it may come back to you in other ways. (SL)

****

This is funny story that only a Dave Ramsey listener will understand.

I have been working on becoming debt free for about 5 years since my divorce.

I have led Financial Peace University at my church for the past five summers.

My commercial building is my final debt and finally after years of praying I have a written contract to sell it on or before January 21, 2020.

The agreed sales price is less that I need to close.

Since I have never missed a payment and should have an excellent credit score, I didn't think it would be a problem to just borrow the difference so I can close.

IN PURSUIT OF THE AMERICAN DREAM

As you all know in FPU we know the first thing I should have tried was selling everything but my kid and absolute necessities to get the difference. I tried to talk myself into thinking that wasn't practical.

I went to my bank that I have done business with for over 10 years. They actually hold the note on my building. I sat down with the lady that knows me pretty well to get a loan for the difference.

Her face turned white and her eyes got really big as she was looking at her computer screen.

I said what's wrong?

She said your FICO score is 0.

I'm not even sure how that can happen while you still have a loan from the bank.

She began to tell me that I should always have a credit card as I began to celebrate and ask if I could take a picture with my 0 FICO score.

I explained that my goal was to have a 0 FICO score and get out of debt. I also told her that I teach people not to have a credit card and that my son and I blew up our last credit card a few years ago.

God answered my question about should I sell my stuff and just be debt free asap. I left the bank laughing.

Now it's time to get to working! Please pray for me as I GET IT DONE!(SM)

****

I just wanted to come on here and do my DEBT FREE SCREAM!!!! My goal was to have all student loans paid off before I was 30 (May 2020) With a lot of hard work and determination we just paid the last loan off 2 nights ago. I don't have many other to brag to. Most roll their eyes and some even told me that it was a waste of money to pay it off when you could just pay minimums forever or defer defer defer (really?)

Regardless I'm very proud and excited and I knew if anyone would understand and be pumped it would be you guys! Onto baby step #3 (and to start working on kiddo #2!) (JN)

****

I know $350 isn't even half of BS1 but I'm so proud of us! This is just from December. I've been selling all kinds of stuff. Including my precious books. Debt free here we come.

I can't wait to start BS2!! (MO)

****

2020 will be my year! My new raise will provide extra funds for debt repayment and sinking funds. I'm on track to pay TWO credit cards off by March based on my worst-case scenario income. Based on worst case scenario, I'll be debt free by 2025!! (CN)

****

Sending out my LAST student loan payment today!!!!
Original payoff date: April 2021!!
Paying it off almost a year and a half early.
Credit card: ☐
Student Loan: ☐
Car: Tackling this next.
I am almost debt free!!
Soo thankful for DR, CH, and ALL of you! **(LB)**

****

"This place is the worst! I'm going home!
Nooo! You can't leave, remember? You'll be broke, out on the streets! But I hate it here. Shut up! Stop being weak! FOCUS"

This is me talking to myself at work this week But I didn't quit! I'm focusing on the BIG GOAL! *Baby noises in the background (MM)

I PAID OFF MY STUDENT LOANS!!!! (WS)

Just paid off my first two debts...not a huge accomplishment but I feel pretty great. This is just the beginning!!! (KD)

****

So this just happened tonight! My friend and I went to Olive Garden for dinner which was budgeted for, I started getting out the EveryDollar app on my phone to put the amount in with my tip and the waitress kept looking at me and I was like yeah we're trying to get out of debt so I use this app it's by Dave Ramsey.

I asked her, "Do you know who that is? She said, "yeah I've heard of him," but she had never seen the app. I told her I absolutely love this app because it does keep me on budget. I could only give her a $10 tip because I didn't have any more money in the budget than that, which was still over 20% but I would've loved to of given her more if I was able to.

What I realized was when she told me "you may have just changed my life," was I gave her something so much more better than a tip. I gave her hope. I gave her the hope that you guys and Dave Ramsey's program gives me every day!

I'm saying all this for everybody to realize that it's not about the presents under the tree it's about being there for others and we can all afford to give hope and smile to others!! Merry Christmas!! (SI)

****

WE JUST CASH FLOWED CHRISTMAS!!
I know...I know...that shouldn't be news but that's the first time in my adult life I've been able to say that! Since that first promo credit card at 18 (I really wanted the cool free shirt) until this year (15 years

to be exact) we have always put something on credit or like last year, spent our emergency fund on gifts.

But nope, not this year! Paid for...in cash! All of it!! (RJ)

Holy Cow!! Somebody tell MURPHY TO BACK OFF!!! The week started with a lice attack, then it was food poisoning for my wife, then it was a flat tire with no jack, then came RSV for my granddaughter, and to top it off, my poor son just got into a wreck. The house is trying to take this all-in stride, but goodness gracious me... I'm about to lose my mind!!! BS2 EF has been tapped into. Still thankful for the steps. Goal: Debt Free in 2020, is still a go. (CH)

****

BS2. For the first time EVER in my adult life (I'm 37 :/) I have made my mortgage payment, 2nd mortgage payment, and car payment in DECEMBER..... I used to make those late and use all that money for Christmas. This year, we budgeted Christmas (and started saving in the summer). Low and behold we're $125 under budget for Christmas, and our big bills are paid on time/early! This will be the first January I won't be scrambling to figure out how to double pay payments or question "OMG - what have I done?!"
Merry Christmas Baby Steppers!! (JK)

****

Final grades are in: I've officially graduated college... DEBT-FREE. (NK)

My husband and I just finished baby step 3 today!! Woohoo!!! next up: 4,5,6 (LR)

****

A breakfast group of 10 or so ladies met for breakfast. Each brought a $100 bill. If I remember correctly, their bill came to a little over $100, total. The waitress was tipped over $1,000! Can you imagine?!

Not sure if this was a Baby Stepper, but it was certainly a group of generous women with kind hearts and a giving spirit.

We did it, WE'RE DEBT FREE!!! Our family of 5 has taken the past 14 months following the Dave Ramsey principals living intentionally and, on a budget, and paid off $60,772.42!!

****

It was not always easy (along with having another baby), but now having crossed the finish line, it was definitely worth it! I'll never forget how mortified i was looking at where all our money was going each month when we did our first budget

Thank you ____ for originally sharing your story, teaching, and motivating us along the way; _____ for all the "free entertainment" and family meals ; and our friends & family for your love and support this past crazy year! On to baby steps 4,5,6!! (DS)

****

In 2020 my debt snowball goes to my final debt—my 401k loan. It's going to be satisfying seeing my net worth increase $1500/mo. Woot woot! (LA)

****

I'm debt FREE! $91,015.91 in 25 months!!!! (CK)

****

Just want to say Merry Christmas Ramsey fans. My last debt is the mortgage, but everyone in this group is trying and I wish everyone Millionaire status someday! Whether you hit it or not, you're sure farther in life than had you never tried. Feel Blessed that you can turn on the radio and get his free advice. It may not be around forever. Dave provides all the direction you need to be successful. I Thank God for him. His teachings have made difference! Don't forget to be generous along the way! (TD)

IN PURSUIT OF THE AMERICAN DREAM

****

on 12/18/2019 (my birthday) My boss called and gave me a $2/Hr raise!!!! Bigger Shovel! (KN)

Four years of sacrifice to end many years of Credit Card misuses. Glad it's finally over. (MC)

****

Who's gonna be debt free in 2020?!?! (AK)
This week my husband had surgery on his ankle and is off for three months, yet today we completed BS#3!! Onward and upward!! YOU, too, can do it! (KK)

****

With still working on BS1 I am on basically a $0 budget for friends and family, so I used what I had. I collected jars from myself and a few friends, grinned fresh coffee beans and topped it off with four coffee filters and twine! Almost all of my family members are huge coffee lovers, so I felt it was perfect, cheap and saved some bottles from the land field (MN)

****

This came in my daughter's backpack today. She's 5 and in Kindergarten. She desperately wants to be "debt free" and has $657 saved in her own account we opened earlier in the year.
We keep telling her she IS debt free, but she says no, no, no, not until she completes Baby Step 1! (AL)

****

Merry Christmas to us!! We've been planning to be under $70,000 in school loan debt by the end of the year, and tonight we put paid off $3,000 of it. We are now at $68,500. We started at $100,000 three years ago and have been taking home >$27,000 a year. My husband just graduated from OT school, and we pray to have that income increasing soon. (AW)

When your boss gives you a gift card for being one of the employees who picked up the most overtime this year...409 hours of OT...she said thanks so much for helping us out so often. I said "Thanks, Dave Ramsey said I had to." LOL #GazelleIntense #DebtfreeByMay2020 (NC)

The absolute best feeling about being debt free and saving up for Christmas, is being able to walk into a furniture store and being able to pick out exactly what we wanted (and more) within our preset budget. Walked out of there stress free! Knowing that we have it paid for and no haunting payments! (HR)

****

OMG... feeling so blessed, God is GOOD! My work nominated us for their holiday Christmas tree and surprised us with an early Christmas. (MS)

****

I was so worried about Christmas this year, I'm so thankful for the community that I work for.

> I'm so poor,
> I rub cologne from
> magazines on my shirt
> When people say,
> Oh you smell good,
> what is that?
> I say, 'Page 14'

He's not a strict DR follower, but my boyfriend paid off his car yesterday!!! He just turned 23, is completely debt free, and is working on moving up in his field So proud of him! (AD)

****

Thou Shalt not turn the heater on until 45° F is achieved. (DE)

Yesterday I stopped at a gas station to fill up my Van. I pulled up to a pump where a young lady was standing behind a very old and kind of beat up vehicle looking at the gas pump, then looking at her phone, then back at the gas pump... she was obviously having some issues.

She finally noticed me sitting there for a minute, so she got in her car and pulled it up to the pump in front of her allowing me to pull up the pump she had already been at. She sat in her car for a minute then she got out again looking at her phone and then back at the gas pump then she got back in her car again and sat there.

At that moment I felt this overwhelming compulsion to speak to her. So I walked up to her car and tapped on the glass. She opened her door because the window wouldn't roll down and looked a little puzzled at me. I told her that God had put it on my heart to pay for her gas that day. She was shocked. She said, "for real?" I nodded and said, "no kidding!" She broke down crying and hugged me.

I could feel the weight on her shoulders as she hugged me. I swiped my card in the pump and told her to fill it up all the way. She gathered herself together and pumped gas into her car. Then I went back to my van and began pumping my own gas. Before I was done, she came over to me and said, "Ma'am you have no idea how much that helped me." She fought back the tears as she said, "I was out of gas but I also have to get my baby's medicine and I didn't have enough money to do both so I been trying to figure out what I was gonna do. Now... wow! You're an angel! Thank you!"

I encourage everyone in this group, who is past baby step 2, to keep your eyes open for someone who might need $20-30 of their groceries paid for, or gas, or just tucked in their pocket as if they "lost" it. Your reward will be bigger than any gift you'll ever receive. (TY)

****

Do you think it would be Dave Approved to get a new toilet? Our toilet exploded last night. We do have a couple of bushes we could use outside, but it's snowy and cold, so we really don't want to go that route. (MT)

When callers don't answer Dave's questions directly, I be like, "Ah! Answer the question! "What is your household income?" "We don't need a 20-minute qualifier." (JB)

****

I've done the smartest or maybe dumbest thing to save money. We just got a new Dunkin Donuts in town and the first 100 people got free coffee for a year. I don't sleep well so I knew I would be awake anyways so I might as well be sitting at Dunkin awake instead of at home. My daughter and I were 13 and 14 in line and both got a year of free coffee plus enough for this month and January 2021 so it's 14 months total. When translated into hours spent, we each earned about $16 an hour in coffee. I would do it again! (VH)

> I love when people in $60k cars want to play road rage with me. My car is worth $986.13 and my life sucks. I will kill us both 😳

The husband and I are in the car arguing about getting gazelle intense in the new year and we looked up and saw the ultimate sign (HH)

I gave Sallie Mae her eviction notice this morning!! Good bye debt! Never again! (NR)

****

Yesterday I received an amazing blessing from one of my clients. (I have a residential cleaning business) He handed me a check and wished me a Merry Christmas. I thanked him and went about my cleaning. I looked at the check a while later and was in shock...$500!!! I went to his wife and said,

"Do you know what he gave me??" And she laughed and said "Money!" I said that is too much!! She hugged me and said "No that's not enough for all that you do for us, you are so much to me! You are a mentor, a friend, a sister in Christ"

I used to hate my job. Cleaning 5-6 toilets a day, mopping floors, dusting etc. it got old. Then God changed my attitude and convicted me with " When you work, work as if working for the Lord and not for man" This has helped me turn my job into a ministry and to take time with my clients and meet their needs on a whole different level.

****

I also have been struggling recently with my tithing as I am in-between church homes right now but had recently sent a large check to a homeless shelter my friend runs in Tennessee.

****

I don't believe tithing is magical, however I do believe God's word and promises are true and in Malachi HE says "Bring the whole tithe into the storehouse, that there may be food in my house. Test me in this," says the Lord Almighty, "and see if I will not throw open the floodgates of heaven and pour out so much blessing that there will not be room enough to store it."

Malachi 3:10 NIV

I wasn't desperate for this money (although I have been in the past) however, I am in baby step 2 and have been struggling to really be gazelle intense. This $500 is going to really help me knock out my smallest debt and free up cash to hit my next one hard. HE is faithful...that's promised. Merry Christmas everyone and thanks for letting me share! This journey is hard at times when you're single and have no accountability. This group helps **(MB)**

Alright, I don't know what to do. My BEST friend is getting married in March of 2021 and is having her bachelorette party in Disney in August of 2020.. (I know) She is planning for a 5-day trip, but I told her I can't take that much time off of work so I will fly down for 3. She wants to spend 2 days at the Disney parks which will be $275 for the tickets. Her Fiancé is paying the lodging costs. And I am also responsible to pay $75 for my half of the car rental. I work in real estate so every month is a fluctuation of income. (No base salary, I could make $0 a month, or I could make a couple thousand.) I'm still a year in so I'm very conservative with my spending habits. I'm not in any debt and I live by my budget but of course I have my monthly bills. Anyway, I'm estimating $300 for a plane ticket after taxes, fees, luggage. Gas to the airport and back $30, and $25 to park my car over the weekend. My grand total before food/drinks/ etc. is $705. I'm thinking after tourist prices I'm going to have to dish out $1000 and I'm stressing out.. I have to go, right? How do I make this a frugal trip??

Edit to add: I cannot drive because I cannot afford to take days off for travel time nor do I want to drive 18 hours by myself. I am self-employed I do not get PTO. Also, she picked the idea of renting a car, and she decided on Disney for two days. (fri-sat) I am also in the wedding, yes. And I DO want to go. I just don't know if I can with my unknown income. I've stayed debt free this far.. but I have living expenses that have to come first. (JH)

****

Today was payday and I had to stare at my bank account because I have more money than I have ever had !! Thanks DR (SL)

IN PURSUIT OF THE AMERICAN DREAM

****

On BS 2 and on a strict budget, I took my sister for Frappuccino for her birthday and someone in front of us (drive thru) paid for our drinks...they must be on BS7...TY anonymous (JD)

You guys I just want to brag on my hubby (Justin L Buckley) for a minute. He works so stinking hard it's amazing. We started the baby steps October 1st this year, with $48,451.29 in debt. We have been constantly chipping away at our debt including $1625.00 in child support (from a crooked post 18th birthday lawsuit) my husband worked so hard that today we sent that child support payment in FULL to his ex-wife, a mere 5 days before Christmas. My husband has cash flowed our entire Christmas shopping this year, helped us stick to all of the budgets. And by December 31st of this year (in 3 short months) we will have paid off $16,862.74 of our debt (that's 33%) now this is with a average household income of only about $45k. We have been working second and third jobs, side hustling, pinching and counting every penny. But we are moving and grooving! We've even put aside our tithing money and we're able to donate to the local dog shelter. We have been living like no one else so that soon we can live and give like no one else. I am so thankful for Dave Ramsey, for his team and the folks in this group! I can't wait to be in Nashville to do our debt free scream this summer!! Stay gazelle intense y'all! (TB)

****

Going through the process to close my credit cards now that all balances are $0. Wanted to share two experiences:

1. Discover fought HARD and tried to convince me to keep the account open even after I dropped Dave's name three times. "That's so great you're on your way to being debt-free, how about we lower your monthly threshold to $500?" No thank you, CLOSE THE ACCOUNT! They finally did.

(Less infuriating but still funny: When I told Wells Fargo I'm working my way toward living debt-free and want to close my account, they said they're sorry for my circumstances and hope things get better. I'm not sure what they thought was going on but I'm not sorry)

2. USAA left my heart full. Spoke to a wonderful person named Tyler and when I explained I'm working on Dave Ramsey's baby steps and very close to being debt-free, they didn't try to convince me or question me or offer any promotions. They moved forward with the process and when I thanked them for not trying to push me otherwise, they said it's not their place to do that when someone has a personal goal in mind. Then they shared they're also a Dave fan currently in BS2! We got to talking and it was one of the most pleasant experiences I've had talking to a stranger on the phone. Thank you, Tyler, for your exceptional customer service and to USAA for not pressuring customers into making detrimental financial decisions.

Hope this helps anyone going through the account closing process. Stick to your guns and your talking points! Now I'm only $16K in two students loans away from being debt-freeeeeeeee! (TS)

****

Cash flowing is vital. Picking up more debt or moving debt around shows behavior. Today I cash flowed $6k to move into a nicer/bigger rental & paid cash for new washer & driers. Tomorrow I will pay cash for 2 new Sealy queen beds. It's always enticing to do 0% financing, but when I made the commitment to not be immature w my $ coupled by my desire to stop the madness I got real! Honest with oneself is vital in the process. God sees it all. Being obedient has brought me into a new realm.

Total debt $94k
Remaining $16k
Believe me, if I can do it...so can u! Lake view from my kitchen. So worth the sacrifices I've made. (JG)

Our tree for this year! We are focusing on our debts, not on materialistic items! Our 4 kids had modest gifts! And, if someone ask me what we want for Christmas I respond gift card for food or

Home Depot card for house fixes. What are you doing or not doing this holiday?

****

I'm on BS2 and decided to buy 1 lottery ticket as a gift for myself....something I don't regularly do. This guy comes in and was also going to buy lottery tickets. He says the last time someone bought the lottery ticket I was going to boy they won $1000. I said to him, well if I win Ill split it with you. Went to the car scratched the first spot and hit for $200. I ran back inside (we were the only 2 customers there) I said don't go anywhere we have a winner. I kept rubbing. I said to him Merry Christmas...we each get $250. We were both so happy....mine is going to pay off my cell phone!!! So happy for I was able to pay it forward and pay a bill!! (CB)

****

How do I tell my husband he needs to be working, not be disrespectful, or tear up our marriage, we aren't making it on just my check.....(AH)

**** I JUST WANTED TO GIVE DAVE RAMSEY THANKS TODAY !!!!!! Ive been sick with the flu for the last 4 days and I wanted to thank Dave because not one time I ever had to call in sick to a boss at a job !!!!! LOL !!!!! I lived like no one else years ago and still do to this day because (I'm a little quirky as you all know) BUT I GET TO LIVE LIKE NO ONE ELSE NOW BECAUSE DAVE BASICALLY RETIRED ME FROM THE TICKING TIME TRAP WORLD CALLED A FULL TIME JOB !!!!! LOL !!!!! So if your new here in the Dave Ramsey world TRUST ME STICK WITH DAVE RAMSEY BECAUSE HE WORKS !!!!! LOL !!!!! He helps you get back the luxury of time in your life !!!!!!**** (DW)

****

For the first time in our marriage we will not be carrying credit card debt into 2020 (JW)

****

My husband isnt too on board with the DR plan when its -25 here in Eastern Canada. Im keeping the heat down 4 points lower than any other year. Told him to wear a sweater.

This is his unhappy protest to my cheapness: **(DH)**

DUMB STUFF WE'VE DONE WITH MONEY

Debt is dumb and cash is king. ~ Dave Ramsey

I had to add this section because most of us really beat ourselves up over the stupid stuff we've done with our money. I want you to realize that you aren't alone. We've all done stupid stuff with our money.

You just have to get over it and move forward. In time, hopefully you can laugh about it and chalk it up to just being young, dumb and stupid. Now that you have been enlightened, are aware of the Baby Step Formula, you have no excuse for being stupid with your money ever again!

I say that tongue in cheek, of course. No one is perfect, even Baby Steppers. I'm sure we will all continue to do stupid stuff with our money, just hopefully not at the same level of stupidity.

It seems vehicles (things with motors), designer accessories and student loans top our list of regrets. I hope you will get a few laughs and amusement out of reading some of the dumb stuff we've done with our money so that you will realize that maybe what you've done isn't quite so bad after all!

I'll start this off by sharing one of the dumbest things I've personally ever done with money:

I spent our rent and utilities money to fly out to California to surprise my new army husband at his first duty station. I was in love and thought I couldn't live another minute without seeing him. He was a private and I was clueless how the military worked. It took us forever to recoup that mistake, but…had a blast and we still laugh and shake our heads over my stupidity.

Vehicles & Toys:

- Financing a 2017 car with negative equity (trade in) never again will I finance a car.
- I bought an 08 escape in 07. I was 18. That was probably terrible lol. I also bought a house that year. The escape was totaled and paid off by insurance and the house foreclosed on. Weird that I think both of those happened the same year too
- Leased a car at not even 18 years old. Went totally over on my mileage when car was due back, owed more money the car was worth Never Again!
- Dumbest purchase? I don't even know. Probably spending twice my truck's value to repair it three months in a row.
- That said, I can't fathom $400 shoes. We all had a vice, I guess.
- In 2009 husband and I both financed brand-new cars. Insanity! Fortunately, both are paid off. I still have mine and husband paid cash for a used vehicle this summer because his died (he drives nearly 2x as much as me)
- I purchased a brand-new vehicle overpriced (cash) but that cash came from home equity loan. Looking back at this wtheck was I thinking!
- Financing two cars paid one off in October and sold it. We are a one car family now. Saving on fuel and insurance. Purchased a $2000 treadmill on credit and the wife has only put about 50 miles on it in 2 years. These are just a few STUPID things we have done. Fixing it now, never to go back!
- My 2017 Jeep Wrangler !!! I had a perfectly good car before I purchased it that was paid off
- Now reading your post— another dumb moment— co-signed a 2018 jeep Sahara $48000 loan. I know my brother will pay but the loan is for 7 years

- Paid off my used 07 Toyota Yaris in 2011. Then...I bought a brand new 2012 RAV4 in March of 2012 cause I had A baby and needed a bigger car, shipped it to the states in July, traded it in for a used 2010 Prius in Dec because it was "too big." refinanced to lower payments. Finally paid it off in April of 2019. Sold it for $5K in Oct.
- No more brand-new vehicles, no more financing ridiculous loans, no more carrying over loan balances ughhh! Smarter decision since we had more babies...put half down on a used 2011 Sienna in Sep 16, financed $7K. Will be paid off in a few months!!
- Leased 3 cars
- A brand-new GMC Acadia. Love the car, hate how much work it has needed and how little it is now worth.
- Traded in my favorite paid for car for a mess used SUV that I completely overpaid for because my ex-boyfriend thought I needed something more reliable in the snow. Hated it. Rolled negative equity into a brand-new car. When it was finally gone, it was worth $9000 and I owed $20,000
- A Mazda CX5 which was a LEMON and had 4 engines in 3 years. Lost all the money we invested in that car thinking it would get us 10 years. Only grateful that we paid cash for it and didn't pay interest as well.
- Financing a 12,300 2016 Toyota Camry 1year and a half ago. I still owe more than the value by like 500.
- I purchased my retirement vehicle, Dodge Durango, brand new, and though I love it, regret it. After having no car payment for a year...smdh...
- I bought (financed) a used $16k car when my income was $32k. It's paid off now but that'll NEVER happen again
- So many cars. Stupid with 0s on the end.
- Some of my more expensive car journeys
- $55k vehicle got rid of it for a $44k vehicle, got rid of if it for 23k vehicle of which 7k was rolled into it from the 44k vehicle. Wised

up and now both of our cars are paid off.
- Brand new car my last semester in college. I wanted a used car but the dealer told me I don't qualify for used, only new... STUPID!
- My dumbest purchase/finance was lease a car with my then bf. I will never again do that again.
- Our van. Had $8,000 negative equity we rolled into a new van purchase 2 years ago ("old" van was only 3 years old).
- Ram 1500 Hemi. It was me, I wanted it. Hubby went along with it. We bought it in June. We don't have a "need" for it, and we have four kids so we can't even fit everyone if we all need to go somewhere. But now we are in our baby steps and chugging away. I wish I could go back and smack myself though.
- Traded in my just about paid for 2012 Mitsubishi Lancer for a 2015 Dodge Journey that's worth nothing now and I still owe $12,000 on it and it's worth like $3000. I thought I needed the space because I had just had a baby. I loved that car hahah
- 10,000 on a bike I bought and literally never used so the engine is done and it's worth nada
- Bought jet skis used for 6,500 stored them at 100.00 month for 2 yr spend 3k on one engine then my friend flooded it sold for 1,200 both bc I refused to pay more storage.
- 30' travel trailer with all the bells and whistles
- Our dumbest purchase was a pop-up camper. We bought it brand new off of the showroom floor. Not even two months after we bought it things started going wrong, things would break or stop working, we took it back to the dealer, they'd put a bandaid on it...
- My husband is one of the people Dave talks about with a bass boat. He has one he bought for $13,000 but it only had a 200 hp engine, so he sold it and bought a $40,000 one with a 250 hp engine. It's currently for sale. Lol

Designer Tags

- 10 years ago, my previous husband was in the military and overseas so we were making pretty good money. I asked him for a pair of Jimmy Choo's for Christmas....$400 ON CLEARANCE!!!! When Dave asks about the dumbest purchase you've ever made as an adult, these shoes come to mind! I live in Wyoming!!! Why did I think these were a smart purchase????
- I won in a raffle from Dillards a 350 dollars Michael Kors purse that I have only used 3 times in 3 years. I will never pay that much for a purse myself post Dave.
- 70 Louis Vuitton bags don't even let me count the Chanel
- I've spent almost $4,000 on two Jimmy Choos purses. But still have them
- I bought a pair of Louboutin's. On a credit card that I did not pay off right away. Fast forward 5 years, my foot grew after having a baby and the damn shoes didn't even fit anymore.
- A 700.00 purse that I love
- 4 different LV bags with matching wallets. I've gotten one stolen but sold 2 (sadly). I still have one I refuse to sell.
- $400 on a pair of Dolce and Gabana shades I had to have bc Naomi had a pair on in an oversized ad in Vogue
- I paid almost $300 for a pair of Ray Bans and lost them a few months later.
- $3k on a Prada purse
- Right along those lines actually! $700 on Laboutins TWICE. The first time I broke my heel because the dumb me went salsa dancing in them! (DUH!) Also a $1200 pair of Prada boots (sold on baby step 2 for a measly $100 and I swear the girl thought it's a sex trafficking scam based on how fast she ran off our porch after picking up the boots and dropping the money in our mail slot), and for the cherry on the top: a $1700 Prada purse purchased in Milan on our (financed) honeymoon. I still have the

purse and can't sell it because it's so sentimental. The kicker? I am a minimalist aspiring for a zero-waste home. I stopped carrying purses 5 years ago!

- I didn't buy (and I have the money) but I wanted a Louis Vuitton bag for $2000 and I don't like to carry a bag. But they are so beautiful
- I love jimmy choos! Now, louboutins are another story - I don't regret mine in terms of money but they're so uncomfortable! I call them restaurant shoes, only good for going to the car, to the restaurant and then back to the car
- My husband bought me this Gucci purse set cause I wanted it so bad like 2,000 dollars have used it like 3 times in 3 years! I love it though! But waste of money.
- I have a beautiful pair of Christian Louboutin pink patent leather heels. I want to wear them, but I swear they sold me the wrong size. I've worn them a few times, but they kill my feet. I'll pass them to my daughter. But we're the worth it? Ha ha no.
- I went through a lularoe phase... so shameful
- $4k on a Chanel bag. Not saying I wouldn't ever buy them but there's a time and a place. Wasn't the right time in ny life for that kind of purchase...and I financed it smh.
- Ya'all's purchases make me feel better! I bought a $400 coach purse about 8 years ago. I don't regret it, it lasted forever and was gorgeous. I'll never do it again though.
- Luxury purses & expensive restaurants
- I had over 60 pairs of Jordans before Ramsey. Needless to say, a majority of those were sold for my Emergency Fund.
- I've been there. I have to laugh to stop from crying sometimes. I spent thousands on shoes and clothes.
- I started "collecting" and "restoring" vintage pieces. Oh, how I love them! I gave 2 friends vintage LV bags I'd re-done for Christmas last year. I regret this
- I was JUST watching a Friends episode where Monica buys some

outrageously priced boots and Chandler is upset about it. She told him they would go with everything and she would wear them every day! She then couldn't hardly wear them bc they hurt her feet so bad. These shoes remind me of that episode! Not saying they're not comfortable but probably would be to me. Lol

- I think my dumbest purchase was a Gucci belt. Cause I don't really wear belts and especially not 350-dollar belts lol
- $550 Tom Ford Sunglasses. All put on a credit card
- I've had 2 pair of Louboutins, a pair of Fendi strappy heels and a pair of Manolo Blahniks all sold on Poshmark when I found Dave. I still have my black Fendi pumps because those are my business meeting shoes. I believe the five pair cost roughly $3000 total and I would buy 5/6 of them again in a heartbeat. So I'm living like no one else so one day I can spend $625 on all the Louboutins I could ever dream of.
- Charged $2000.00 worth of gym clothes. Seriously stupid, you sweat in them. No one cares how you look when you sweat, good grief!
- 2 purses one LV and one Gucci…over 7k
- Mine is just countless small clothing purchases that add up over time and most of it I don't even wear
- My current leased vehicle and all the material clothes, shoes and accessories I "needed." Happy to have found this group to start actually saving!

Education

- $40000 in student loans
- High school diploma course. been stuck on one essay for almost 2 years. And last year I told my husband I wanted adidas, pink adidas shoes. I never wear them $170 for nothing
- A Specialist degree that will not get me the job I thought I wanted. I should have done National Board Certification instead. Much cheaper and greater benefit.
- Mine would be 40k in student loans and I still don't have a degree. Still going back and forth about going back and finishing. All the jobs I want even though I have the experience they won't hire me bc I don't have a Bachelors.
- Cosmetology school. I get 50% off professional hair products though!! Only cost me $13,000 and growing with interest.
- Student loans and then leasing a car when my car died when I literally had an emergency fund to fix/buy a cheap car and I DIDNT use it for the emergency! Lol
- 25k student loan I've only made minimum payments on since 2002 Its a federal loan so the interest it's accrued since then is 4 k which has fueled the complacency about the loan. I'm gearing up to hit them hard and finally be done with it
- Student loans were the dumbest financial choice I've EVER EvER made. My husband and I have been on the debt free journey and getting the kids (well basically raising the kids in it to avoid even getting into debt) and want to involve the family.
- 15 or 20k over about 3 years for energy healing school and related expenses. (30 years ago). An expensive lesson. Though I don't regret it totally bc I did learn a lot. But sometimes I think about what if I had invested that $.
- My graduate school experience- I never finished this particular degree and didn't really want the degree. Talk about a STUPID tax.

Food:
- I financed a hamburger once.
- I continue to spend about $20-$22 a day to get Postmates food delivered at work when I could just run across the street and get subway for $6...or I could pack a lunch
- Restaurants. $1000+ a month! (Family of 3) & purses. Not crazy expensive ones, but a LOT of $50 ones! Several a month or more.
- I'd probably say my worst financial mistake has been eating out all these years. I don't even want to think about how much it all totals up to.
- Groceries and fast food on credit. I can't show you...it's gone. Seriously though... dumb dumb dumb. Financing food. SMH at myself.
- I have a whole bunch of them. Mostly because every apple I have to throw because I bought too many and couldn't eat them in time and every second ice-cream box goes to that category. The devil is in the tiny details. And I have many tiny details that I regret at the end of a month when my groceries budget is $40 over.

Furniture/Appliances
- A $4K mattress
- I bought a Tempur Pedic.
- Bought an adjustable bed with my ex for 4500 and I ended up getting to pay it off and he kept the bed. It was so firm, I hated it anyways
- Probably our $2200 couches. Comfy, but could have found cheaper. Cash flowed. But still.
- A $700 "baby tenda" crib. It was our first baby and the crib "grows with them". That was 16 years ago. Said baby plus her 3 siblings ALL slept in that crib and never once did we "convert" it to a toddler or day bed. I guess we got our money out of it...but had to have 4 kids to do so
- I spent $1000 on a giant bean bag. And I financed it. But its soooooo comfy.

- An expensive new couch, which my kids and dogs have totally destroyed.
- BMW, brand new furniture
- The bins that go under front loading washers/dryers
- I financed a couch. With USB ports and all lol
- A booth table for our basement. Big, bulky, uncomfortable, plain old dumb.

Vacuum Cleaners:
- A vacuum cleaner from one of those door to door salesman. I'm still horrified 15 years later. Filter queen. 2,500. Cash I had been saving up for my wedding. They showed us giant blown up pics of dust mites and convince you they are taking over the household and without the vacuum you're doomed. My sales gal was about 18 and looked like she lived out of her car. We still joke that was likely her only sale.
- Delpin vacuum. We were poor, newly married young people who got suckered into thinking a $1200 vacuum that used water instead of a bag was the way to go. Plus it was a pain to actually use. We listed it online for a long time and ended up throwing it in a dumpster before a move.
- $4000 rainbow vacuum
- Rainbow vacuum... and we paid cash.
- Kirby Vaccum..... it cost more than my engagement ring

Health & Beauty:
- Gym memberships
- $300 Annual Gym Membership while I was working the graveyard shift and didn't use it
- All my 'diet' gigs
- A Nordic Track elliptical machine with all the bells and whistles and I swore it wouldn't end up collecting dust or become an expensive clothes hanger....well, I will be trying to sell the dust bunny this week on FB marketplace!
- A treadmill for our finished attic. Made the whole house (built in 1929) shake. Eventually we had to pay someone to take it apart and get it down two flights and out so we could give it away.

- A bunch of workout DVDs lol
- $800 at Ulta in one transaction
- A massage and seaweed wrap at the MGM Grand for $400.... so stupid!
- $10,300 for laser hair removal. All financed. The dumbest part is I could have gotten it waaaay cheaper. It was definitely a dumb decision!
- My dumbest purchase: weight loss surgery. It was expensive (insurance doesn't cover bariatric surgery in my state) and I never met my goal weight, didn't even get close. Never had GERD, until I had bariatric surgery, still struggling with infertility. Just not happy with myself.
- Hair extensions! They look great but my gosh not necessary.
- $500 on make up to help me look younger - never used

General:

- Not a dumb purchase but dumb choice. I would give my mom money and she would just gamble it away. Which I knew about because I was 15 when she started asking me for it. She would get $425 a month for child support and made $20+ an hour at her job.
- When we were dating my husband bought tickets to see Ed Sheeran because I mentioned I liked a couple songs on an album that came out. I think it was right after the Ariana concert shooting. We didn't end up going because #1 neither of us actually like Ed Sheeran that much and #2 we were kind of freaked out by the shooting. The tickets were a little over $300 and they went to waste.
- PS4. I realized after a few weeks of buying it that I don't have the time to play with it. Friend asked to buy it from me 60% of what I paid for it, and I stupidly agreed. I swear I'll never buy a gaming console ever again!
- I moved 12 times in over 10 years. I experienced a lot, so I don't necessarily regret it, but man that was not cheap.
- A Baby Lock jet flow serger sewing machine and everything with it for $1,200. Used it a few times and now can't give it away.

IN PURSUIT OF THE AMERICAN DREAM

- Spent $600 on a custom-made surfboard for my son before he really learned to surf. He ended up needing a different board.
- I bought a plastic tub for $50 - essentially a pail - for an infant bathtub called the Tummy Tub. My husband laughs about it still.
- A swimming pool. The gift that keeps costing us money year after year.
- Anything with the comment "It's only....$xx.xx"
- However, I have a multitude of other really DUMB adult purchases. The year I spent $3000 on Christmas gifts, mostly for our 3 kids. Guess what? Not a single care is give to that Christmas today, did not build character, and the joy was so so so short lived, but the debt lived on.
- Stupid men who just wanted my money
- Wedding! Wish we kept it small and spent the money on a nice trip instead or invested in our future.
- All of my dumb purchases are horse related. Although, they do keep me active and upright which is really important with my health issues they are my biggest blind spot. 9 months with no horse was horrendous. So I went to buy one cheap one (a young untrained one to give me a project) and I came back with two. Thankfully, after putting in some training, I was able to sell one for more than I bought both of them for, but with all the time I put into her I probably broke even.
- Too many to count! last year my husband and I got tickets to this event on governor's island. sort of like a Halloween / interactive performance art and it was $400 a ticket. Thankfully it was a complete sh*tshow, overcrowding and fire code issues left and right so we got refunds. but with drinks/getting to the ferry and such it was basically $1000 night.
- A $500.00 camera I have used ONCE
- A timeshare!
- $1200 for 2019 WNFR tickets!! Paid cash!!! And will do it again. Senseless purchase yes. But omg front row seats above the chutes. Heck yes baby!!! And that is not a zoomed in pic!!!! Y'all have your shoes I like cute cowboys!!!(ps happily married x20 years!!!)
- $800 credit card that I gave to my 27-year-old boyfriend when I was 18 years old. Big mistake.

IN PURSUIT OF THE AMERICAN DREAM

- A $2000 stainless steel Ducane propane gas grill (bought in 2002 not adjusted for inflation).
- 2000$+ on Royal prestige dishes
- When I was 19, I had my first apartment. It was right down the street from a laser tag place. I played laser tag every single day. I was often number 1 on the leaderboard. For some reason my 19-year-old self found this to be a prestigious accomplishment. I also got evicted from my apartment because I spent all of my rent money. On what, you may ask...well, laser tag, of course
- $7500 water softener
- Vending machines that were supposed to make me money but ended up digging me into huge debt.
- I've been frugal my whole life! but did ruin my credit many many years ago getting a cell phone for a BF who of course didn't pay the bill. This was before unlimited minutes, so the bill was like $700
- My third husband.
- I bought lottery tickets. With a credit card. Lots of them.
- A built-in pool and a 60k Audi. That money could have been in mutual funds now making money! I only WISH my mistake was $400!
- After 10 years of marriage I felt like I deserved a new ring. My first was perfectly fine. Beating myself up now that I should have waited until we could pay cash.
- So, not that I would have changed anything, but my biggest financial booboo was living in Manhattan for two years while in grad school. Cost me $20,000 in extra student loans. That decision however did make it possible for me to study, have a space away...
- $15k of video camera gear put on a credit card
- $200 air freshener controlled by phone app
- yeah, I rigged my entire house up with those Phillip's hue lights just so I can say "Alexa turn lights on" lmao!
- Probably financing a filter system for my air conditioning at home. Supposed to help with allergies. But 600$ until it's paid off!

IN PURSUIT OF THE AMERICAN DREAM

- I am not an "image" guy and all my toys have been purchased used.
  So for me I guess it is anything and everything that I bought with a credit card.
- Upgraded touring Broadway tickets so we had good seats to see Hamilton
- I bought tons of house decorations for every single room, but I don't rent or own a home. We live in my in laws basement
- Trips to the beach and Branson. Christmas was always overboard and on CC. I did stupid well.
- Thousands of dollars at QVC!!
- Snowboards. Definitely the snowboards. We were going to Colorado every year skiing or snowboarding so we thought they would get used a lot & be worth it. We live in Oklahoma. That was before kids. We've used them 1x. & bc of where we live there's 0 interest in buying them. So in the closet they sit. so dumb
- I put our home down payment on a credit card.... oof. First time admitting that. I travel a ton for work and they make you pay for everything and then they reimburse you... so I put all my travel on a credit card, then they reimbursed me, and instead of putting that towards the card I used the cash for a down payment.
- I have bought foolish things for sure. I am 60 raised three boys a stepson a niece and now a granddaughter. However, I have never spent money on rainbow vac, I have never owned a pair of shoes that were more than 50.00, never had a purse over 25.00. 80% of clothing is second hand even when I worked. I just upgraded my acrylic paints from Walmart brand for 37.00 and I feel so bad for spending that.
- We haven't really made a whole lot of dumb purchases, just mismanaged. Hubby bought me $2K diamond aascher earrings, but I had them appraised: $4500. I wear them every day. But they were purchased on credit so that was DUMB!
- Mine would be the first pack of cigarettes AFTER I had quit for a year
- $8000 on bicycles plus accessories (helmets and bags)
- Matching Bows for an ex and myself lol. I ended up selling mine, I think he still uses his. Who knows.

- Yes, I remember the CRV with a built-in picnic table, my selling point. Newly married and never had a NEW car…did I hated that thing
- Oh, let's not forget the members only membership for 4500, but it was going to save us so much money when we renovated our house, yeah never used it once.
- I'm gonna wait for someone comment but, my husband bought a commercial grade ice cream machine for the house just before summer. Till this day I'm still kinda upset about it
- Our current house. We went from fully paid off to paying mortgage and land payment. We could have been saving so much money and my husband could have been in a much less stressful job now.
- So…. My birthday is in January and I've asked my husband for an Apple Watch. I keep thinking about this page and how that's $400 I could put towards student loans!
- A time share. Seriously the dumbest moment of my life. Paid it off, paid ridiculous annual maintenance fees, never used it because it cost me to book something, and then paid to "donate" it. Dumb dumb dumb! But we are wiser now and it changed our habits greatly.

Pets:
- Financed a dog because my husband wanted it.
- We bought a $4,000 bulldog at a pet store. We loved him, but he died of blood cancer and wasn't even two years old.
- My dumb purchase was a dog. My dog of almost 7 years had just passed away after being hit by a car and I was devastated so to cope I thought it would be a good time to get a dog from the shelter. I paid $200 for the dog plus easily another $150 to get her everything she needed once we got home. I didn't have time to retrain a dog, and I didn't really have the money I spent either. I ended up giving her away to a friend about 2 weeks after adopting her.

I'M DEBT-FREE

We had the pleasure of making the trip to Nashville to do our debt free scream yesterday! It was such an amazing experience to meet Dave and his wonderful team. (we were on the 3rd hour of the 12/16 show; at the 30-minute mark.)

Our debt free journey has been soooo long! And we barely scratched the surface of all of our run-ins with murphy on our segment. But let me tell you it is so worth it. Keep fighting and pushing through folks! ☐

What time is it? Time to be free!
3... 2... 1... We're debt free!!! (TB)

****

We did it! My husband and i just graduated college debt free! A combination of scholarships, working part time, selling our second car, donating plasma, and budgeting got us to this point. We know the baby steps work! (NT)

****

IM DEBT FREEEEEEEE!

I paid off $51,732.14 in a little less than 16 months. I found Dave Ramsey at the end of July 2018 and followed his plan. It's changed my life. This debt doesn't include murphy slamming into me (my dog passing away, my car needing over $1,000 in repairs, 4 new tires, health issues, health procedures, and getting Ramsey (yes i was that intense that i named my puppy after Dave Ramsey). Those were all on top of the debt. I was able to handle it all though. I worked 3 jobs, 65-75 hour weeks. In the last 3 months, i picked up a 4th job and was working over 80 hours a week. I drained savings accounts and extra things that are no no's in Dave's eyes.

I am so thankful for Dave Ramsey. I went to FPU in January 2019 and went again this fall and was able to do my debt free scream the other week before class started.

I've been so afraid to post I'm debt free on my personal page because I'm afraid somethings going to happen, murphy might come around again and there are so many unsupportive family and friends on there. Find your support system and stick with them! A great support system is key!

I had to post on here though! I even got a shirt to commemorate this!!

Baby step 3 I'm coming for ya! Thank you, Dave Ramsey, I plan on visiting you one day to personally thank you for giving me motivation and hope (RE)

****

OFFICIALLY DEBT FREE!! (NA)

****

I'm debt free! I paid off $21,738.32 in 10 months! It all started when a determined and headstrong woman name ____ came into my life. She would not stop talking about Dave Ramsey and the goal of being debt free. I grew up in poverty and always struggled with money, so being debt free seemed too far out of reach. One day, after feeling broke from paying my car note, she said "imagine not having to owe anyone"... and it hit me like a ton of bricks! "Yes, that would be nice!". Ever since then, her words were no longer going in one ear and out the other (sorry ____). I promised I would post this picture of us when I become debt free, taken December 2018. I can never thank you enough, love you girl! (CS)

****

I'm jumping for joy while (admittedly) holding my breath: I just booked my reservation to join Dave and co. In the 1st debt-free cruise!!! Debt-free was too far out of reach for me to even consider when it was first announced, but when he announced, the past couple days, that rooms had become available, I realized that I am now able to be among that group and I had the cash to pay for it! It's close, but I decided this was the way I wanted to spend that money. I'll have to squeeze the final session of FPU that I will be leading in before I have to leave, but I trust that can get worked out. I am, literally, shaking! I have never made this kind of snap decision involving so much money before. I hope you won't criticize me for needing to share this victory, but I really have no other support system with whom I can. Godspeed to you, all. Dave's plan and our individual efforts do work (ST)

****

We are officially DEBT FREE!!!

We started our debt free journey in Aug 2018, 15 months ago with over $130k of debt between student loans, auto loans, and consumer debt. Household income started at $115k and grew to 137k since then. Our goal was to be debt free in 18 months!

We decided to sell our big beautiful country home on land, to purchase a just-right home closer to hubby's work. The sale of the house paid all but student loans, a lot of luck right there because we were able to sell for way more than we bought.

Hubby sold his big fancy truck and got an old gas efficient Honda sedan. Overage went to debt. Between the Honda and being closer to work, we saved monthly on gas (and insurance).

We sold everything that wasn't necessary; some larger sacrifices (my epic vinyl record collection), some poor-choice spending sacrifices (hot tub, jewelry, farm toys).

We stopped eating out <—- this was huge. We saved so much money by meal planning and *intentional* (stick to the list!!) grocery shopping.

We stopped "retail therapy" shopping, the "we have enough income for more debt" mentality, and the "out-earn the spending" race.... and are living life happily on a moderately strict budget. We buy second hand wherever we can - and only for necessity.

This program has changed the way we view money and spending - to the point of now we are tiny-homing it on a family's driveway while we self-contract/build our "good enough" forever home. Now that we've gotten this far, we simply can't stand the idea of taking out a huge loan for an amount that we'd need to pay on till we retire. We never would have thought like that 2 years ago.

We tithe, and our tithes have gone up since starting this program. Our tithes support our local community as well as teaching the good news of Jesus in other countries. God has blessed us with random money surprises left and right for our faithful giving. Now that we are out of debt, we are going to up the tithe some more

Now we start BS3 without a mortgage (will have a small construction loan soon). We will definitely be everyday millionaires in years to come. We are excited for the opportunity to use wealth to help others, in hugely impactful ways to better our country/world and help the oppressed and poor. Money is power and we will do amazing things with it. God, keep us from greed and corruption, amen.

We do have a big shovel, but we have a bigger hustler mind-set. Nothing will stop us now! Thank you, Dave, for this program. And of course, the biggest thanks goes to the big guy in the sky. We feel free! (MGD)

****

Happy Thanksgiving and Happy Debt Free Day. Today after 2 years and 11 months we woke up debt free. Yesterday was our very last debt payment ever. After purchasing a brand-new travel trailer in January of 2017 because of a babysitting job that would make the payments until the mom quit her job. I knew something needed to change but didn't know where to start. With tax season fast approaching I didn't want to get into the same rut. So I googled "what to do with a tax refund". Up popped a video of Dave explaining the 7 Baby Steps. I put the baby to bed and sat to watch the 1 video. Everything sounded so simple. I told my husband about it and he said do what you want with the money. I just make it and you spend it. Off I went to budget for the very first time. $43,078.21 in debt making $45k up to $55k (thanks to a part time job) and back down to $46k after a military move. Hubby became fully on board about 6 months after finding the video. Lots of struggles along the way after completing Baby Step 1. Two vehicles needed repairs within 1 week, 2 deaths in the family, Big Navy taking 2 months of half months pay. Selling the travel trailer after 2 years of holding onto it. I'm so happy to be free of payments. We have 3 years until hubby's military retirement. We will be completing BS3 in 6 months then moving to 3B up until retirement. (BK)

WE'RE DEBT FREE!

Hard work does pay off!! Over the past 25 months we have paid off all of our student loans, $233,955. The best place to go when you are in debt? To work!

We have worked extra jobs (7!), have made budgets every month, and have said 'no.' We have been blessed with work opportunities and with our friends and families who understood the sacrifices we were making. We are so grateful for Dave Ramsey, the baby steps community, and the podcast which encouraged us to keep going when we were worn out.

You've got to live like no one else so later you can live and give like no one else! (KH)

****

WE'RE DEBT FREE!!! $127,787.99 paid off in 22 months!!!

We began with a huge IRS bill, credit card debt, student loans, a HELOC, an auto lease, medical debt, a Jared credit card for the previous year's Christmas gift and cell phones payments. It even took us almost a year to start using a written budget. We scratched, clawed, fought, sold, bargained, sacrificed, and said a lot of "No" and our kids' usual reply was, "It's not in the budget?" I took in sewing jobs, started a part time job helping a neighbor, I captioned for Rev briefly and we cut everything extra out -- lawn service, pool service, gym membership, tons of eating out/takeout, cable, cell phone adjustments and even had our broken stove fixed because I wouldn't take no for an answer when I called about a warranty issue.

This past spring, something "clicked." We are both self-employed (he's a Realtor and I'm a Massage Therapist) and have mortgages on two rental homes in addition to our primary home. Well, we decided to sell our Denver townhome (the most equity) -- it closed today and we funded our emergency fund and paid off our last debt (the Audi, which was another bit of "stupid" within our BS2 jaunt) in about 5 minutes total as soon as the wire transfer came in. We are also setting aside a huge chunk to pay down this house, as well as upgrade a vehicle for me.

Here is something to consider: If you're chugging through BS1 or BS2, please know that your intensity and hard work will pay off! Don't stop now!!! No matter the size of your shovel, when you start living this new way of life with intent and determination, the finish line will be closer with every breath. Give yourself some grace, as well. We were extremely skeptical, scared, overwhelmed and wanted to quit. It took a minute to completely convince my free-spirit, spending husband that we needed to stick to the budget (I'm the nerdy saver) and not order in because it was "easier." I have to give him a shout though, because I think not long ago I heard him ask about discounts when paying for something.

Way to go, baby, WE DID IT!!! (JT)

****

Our "side gig" made us over $16,200 so far this year! I remember in January feeling defeated because my brother in law made fun of us for reselling. But today, I'm feeling empowered to do twice as much next year! (AC)

****

Today we changed our family tree! We paid off our mortgage and officially became debt free!!! I am beyond grateful for this experience. The best is yet to come

Edited

Our journey began in 2013 after we purchased a truck. My husband came home about 6 months after we purchased it and said he's been listening to Dave Ramsey and we need to sell it! Needless to say I thought he was crazy. After listening to iHeartRadio-Dave Ramsey station I was hooked. In 2015 we paid off our $34,000 truck. Quickly went into BS 3 within 6 months and Bs 4-5-6. We refinanced the mortgage to a 15 year in 2015. We cash flowed several things including a kitchen remodel and the birth of our new baby. In 2018 we decided to pay off our final debt- our mortgage and it has been the most rewarding experience!

A total of $134,000 in a total of 6 years and we're debt free!!!!

****

We paid off our mortgage yesterday! It took us 7 years. DEBT FREE (RF)

IN PURSUIT OF THE AMERICAN DREAM

My wife and I did it! We are COMPLETELY debt free, as well as mortgage free by 27 making less than 100k a year!

We paid off $50K worth of student loans and a car in two years.

After this milestone, we felt the next thing we wanted to do was reduce our housing expense as much as possible in order to live like no one else sooner.

However, we really didn't like the idea of getting in tons of debt again to buy a home in the Portland area (decent homes start about $350k). We just really loved the peace and freedom that being debt free brought.

Therefore, after much contemplation, we decided to purchase a cheap 3b/2bath manufactured home in cash! This decision brings our rent (land-rent) down to only 8% of our income, compared with the original 25%. We plan to invest that difference!

This financial independent journey is so possible guys! It looks different for everyone, but that's the beauty of it! You get to choose the life you want to live!

I encourage you to stay determined, follow the process, and think outside the box! I promise it is so worth it!

Thank you, Dave - for helping my wife and I wake up! You've showed us how to be better stewards with our money, and how to take back control of our life.

***Update

Thank you so much for the kind words everybody

Here are some answers to questions I received.

Range of income : 55-90k the past 3 years.

Work:

Me - Project Manager and Wedding Photography

Wife - Nursing Assistant and Wedding Photography

A few things we did to pay of our debt sooner?

- We tithed and did our best to put Jesus first in our lives and make sure our decisions lined up with his word.

- Established a vision and goals with my wife so we were on the same page. We also spent time together reading personal development books and studied what the Bible says about marriage and finances. A solid team who is clear on the vision and roles is unstoppable.

- We established a budget (Used Mint and EveryDollar) and focused on paying off one debt at a time.

- we reduced housing costs as much as possible. One year, we reduced our rent from 1,500 to 1000 to pay off debt faster.

- We learned a new skill to to serve more people, which in turned generated more income. I learned video and photography. (Don't go into debt to start a business)

- Wife loves to cook. She also took cooking courses and read ebooks so she could become better. We love to eat home cooked meals. (JV)

****

We can officially say WE'RE DEBT FREE! Over the last 16 months we've paid off nearly $68,000 in consumer debt, that we've racked up over the course of our relationship being "normal". We have sacrificed so much, but to us it was well worth it. Our next and final hurdle is to be mortgage free before 2021, but I know we can do it! Thanks to our close friends _____ for encouraging us to join in on their journey! Also to our families for the support and not thinking we were totally crazy. (MB)

****

Just mailed my final house payment today!! Got the house in August of last year, and decided to go crazy working and selling stuff to pay it off in a year! Feels so good to be DONE! Babystep 7, here I come!! (JJ)

IN PURSUIT OF THE AMERICAN DREAM

LIFE OF A BABY STEPPER
WHEN MURPHY COMES CALLING

As I've said previously, Murphy comes to visit each one of us from time to time. No one is immune. Sometimes it feels like he has taken up permanent residence in our Guest Room!

The best thing you can do to protect yourself is to have an adequate emergency fund, which is Baby Step 1: Save $1.000.

Most of the time, this will be enough to take care of the emergency. Sometimes it won't be. If you don't feel confident, just boost your fund up just a little.

If you have older appliances or live in an older home, one thing you should consider is to create a line item in your budget to set aside a few dollars each month to replace things when they go out, because you and I both know, chances are very good that something is going to go out and it will never be at a convenient time.

Here's a few Murphy tales I've read recently from Baby Steppers.

I've seen a lot of posts about Murphy hitting, which is especially hard this time of year. Sometimes these hard things are blessings in disguise that put us on a road to better, but we just must wait out the storm before we can look back and see how much we've grown. Here's our Murphy Story...

Within a month of starting Baby Step 2, we had two major car repairs to do. We preserved though and with all our side hustles were able to replenish our emergency funds and still pay off my husband's car. I paid the car off Tuesday, received the Title in the mail Saturday, our teenage son totaled it Sunday.

We weren't too sure where we would go from there but had peace for the first time in years knowing we would make it through if we just kept at it. The insurance settlement ended up being a tad bit more than we expected. With that, we ended up buying a 1K beater, and used the rest to pay off our second snowball 8 months early, plus it was also our largest monthly payment other than our mortgage.

This really has gotten the ball rolling for us and given us energy and hope. I know Murphy is different for each person, and sometimes takes longer to see the silver lining, but hang in there. I know next time Murphy comes knocking, I'll hang onto this story as I try to wade through it. I can honestly say that I am grateful our son totaled a car! (jg)

****

Soooo. . . .I hit a catfish on the way home from my mom's tonight. Thank you to Brandi Barrow and Stuart Barrow for coming to help me and finding the fish. . .because really who would believe me if I didn't have the fish. (RW)

****Explanation****

A bird dropped the fish onto my car.

****

In October, I finished baby step 1, on Halloween, my vacant rental property flooded for the 2nd time this year. Goodbye ef. Still trying to recover from the 1st flooding incident.

****

Murphy hit me- I first found out my unemployment benefits were overpaid- so I wrote a check for $1190 and used my emergency fund and ALL Christmas money- then I lost my biggest side hustle contract (I am a freelance media planner/ web designer,) lost a $15K contract for 2020. So yeah my week is just sucking- need some love. (GP)

****

Apparently, Murphy wants to be my BFF this year. I keep trying to decline his company, but he jumps in like a 3rd wheel.

We get our son recovered from his accident, and then BAM! "Hello! It's me, Murphy coming to say hi!"

My husband developed pancreatitis from an apparent gallstone. And his liver enzymes went up to a not so good level. Right before I'm set to go back to my work after 3 months of being a caretaker. He's barely been there since August. I'm ready to get aggressive with his doctor/s because he can't live like this.

I start back at work and here comes Murphy again. Corneal erosion in my right eye (yes that eye had been previously injured), almost recovered from that. And I back to work. Well, wouldn't you know it here comes Murphy for another visit. My eye started to get painful and sensitive again. Eye exam showed normal. Saw my Neurologist (I have MS) wants to schedule an MRI. Get to Sunday and started developing a rash on my forehead and right eyelid. It spread to the right side of my head. Today little blisters started to form. It's shingles, shingles on my face and eye. Another missed day of work. And playing things by ear for tomorrow.

Every time this year I get back to work and something happens. Whether it's my heart, my MS, my son falling out of a window, or my husband getting very ill.

It's beyond frustrating and at this point I'm just tired. The blessing right now is that even though we have $4.00 to our names I hit my deductible. I didn't have to pay copays for visits or prescriptions.

And before anyone says anything, yes, I'm trying to sell some of our stuff. I need gas money and money for other family members medications. And we have gotten help with food. Our pantry and fridge are stocked.

If you got this far, thanks for reading. I just needed to rant. I'm trying to let go of the negative and keep pushing forward. I will keep striving for progress with faith that things will get better. I know one day my family will be debt free too. (AE)

Something wonderful happened! Murphy visited our house.

IN PURSUIT OF THE AMERICAN DREAM

Now, when Murphy visit it's never really a good thing, but this time it was different in a way. I have been with the most wonderful man for nearly 15 years and Murphy has hit us hard a few times. Murphy came in the form of two wonderful, beautiful daughters when we were very young. Murphy came in the form of car accident sometimes. Murphy came in the form of home invasions sometimes. Every time Murphy came, we reacted.

We counted on debt to help us get through until we were in a better place. The thing is though, we were never really in a better place. We did eventually make more money yes. We did eventually move away from such a high crime area, yes. But we never got to a better place spiritually, relationally, or financially.

This time, Murphy showed up in the form of a dead washing machine. We hit the laundromat for about two weeks while deciding what to do. We saved up cash and bought a new washing machine deciding that this was an emergency. We set our debt snowball back two weeks in order to do this.

Why is this wonderful?

Because we both agreed that it was not an option to buy the washing machine on a credit card. We also both agreed not to react in the moment and find a solution until we could save up the cash. We also both agreed that it was OK to spend money to get a new appliance that we will need for the next 10 years. So this time when Murphy showed up my husband and I came together as a couple and found a solution that did not involve debt. It was expensive and we really did not want to spend the money like this, but I am so grateful for having found the baby steps because it has brought my relationship, which was already good to A whole new level. (WS)

****

Murphy Hit. Our dryer crapped out. And our washing machine had been shredding our clothes and towels like a cheese grater for the past year. But with being on Baby Step 2 paying down our debt it seemed like a faraway dream to get a new washer and dryer. Old me would have panicked, probably bought new ones on credit then spent money going out to a restaurant to eat and drink away our blues.

The broken part for our dryer would have cost $100+ to get it shipped from a discount parts store online. New me has a sinking fund for home maintenance. New me knows I can pay cash for used stuff. New me and hubby have been side hustling lots. Today me didn't even have to touch our home maintenance sinking fund because we have been side hustling enough this month that we could straight up cash flow a washer and dryer by negotiating a deal to buy this new-to-us set for only $160 Hubby is a handyman by trade and has the new pair already set up washing a load of laundry.

Screw you, Murphy. We've got Dave Ramsey in our corner (JB)

****

Oh Murphy, it's like you heard my excited projections to say goodbye bye to Discover this month as me laying out the welcome mat and calling you to dinner.

First it was the car. Now the waterlines in the green house burst.

I'm afraid to ask what next. (GR)

****

Currently in BS2 & Murphy keeps on hammering at our door... last evening our fridge died (we were down to a small bar fridge). Pre DR I would have purchased one on some form of credit...

I recalled my neighbor previously offering us the use of her spare fridge. Today she 'gifted' us her spare fridge. In return my partner is attending to some home repairs for her.

DR has changed the way I respond & challenged my behavior towards money.

Blessed to have such a kind & generous neighbor.

****

Murphy hit today.

This morning/last night my car was broken into. Luckily they only got maybe 2 dollars in change that I had in my cup holder however they must have gotten angry I didn't have anything they wanted so they decided to slice up my leather seats (my paid off car) with a knife. They hit my whole neighborhood HARD. I was the only one with sizable damage, but some people lost valuables.

I did make a call to my insurance and my deductible for vandalism is $250 ....(the silver lining) today at work, I Unexpectedly got a Christmas gift from my crew of $100.

I would much rather not have to deal with insurance, quotes, etc and throw the extra $100 towards bs2 and not take $150 out of our emergency fund - but it could always be worse. No matter what Murphy throws at you keep going y'all! God is good! Hope everyone is having a great day (JM)

****

Not crazy but sad. Taking my family to my home country for my Uncle's funeral after his sudden death at the start of this year. Cost us over $3k, but due to our emergency fund, this was not what we worried about. And my family appreciated our coming very much. (TS)

****

Friday at 545am driving to work and 2 tires came BARRELING out of nowhere (dark highway) and obliterated my headlight assembly. Thankful it didn't get my windshield. The whole incident took about 1 second from the time it flew at me to hitting me. Didn't have time to hit the brakes. Got a guy behind me too. (CC)

****

Within one month of finishing baby step 2 my dryer broke, found the car I had bought has a rusted frame, and I shattered my phone screen. Good times lol. (EA)

LIFE OF A BABY STEPPER
101 SIDE HUSTLES

Opportunities are everywhere you go; you just must keep your eyes and ears open to see them. Side hustles are great for earning extra cash and sometimes you can hit a goldmine and make so much cash that you have the choice to replace your primary income job!

Sometimes all you need is a spark to ignite a great idea. One idea helps you generate another one even better.

You don't necessarily have to go back to school, you can use what you know right now to start a side hustle. What are hobbies and special interests? Your skills, knowledge, abilities, education and experience? What have you been through that others would pay to NOT experience?

Do you have a knack for bringing people together? Use your skills to connect people to one another, to businesses, products and services.

Are you crafty? You might be able to turn your creations into cash. Computer and tech savvy? Help those who aren't. Think helping the elderly with their smart phones and computers.

Struggling between profit and philanthropy? You can do both.

Owning a family business sound intriguing? Some parents involve the whole family in their ventures.

I've scoured the internet, read tons of articles and books to come up with a list of side hustle ideas that I think will be beneficial in helping you to find the perfect side gig to bring in some extra cash.

Contact me to include your side hustle ideas, pictures and affiliate links in an upcoming or revised edition of this book or to be featured on my podcast.

IN PURSUIT OF THE AMERICAN DREAM

1. Doordash & Instacart
2. Uber & Lyft
3. Fast food delivery
4. Uber Eats
5. Deliver for Amazon Flex
6. Restaurant Server, Waiter, Bartender
7. Tutor Elderly on using their smart phones, social media and computers.
8. Wedding Officiant
9. Test/Reviews (usertesting.com, trymyui.com)
10. Dairy Calving Pen PT Job
11. Social Media Community Manager: Take care of small business owner's social media accounts
12. Merchandise by Amazon - Create designs, upload, receive royalties from each sale.
13. Sell items on Ebay or Craigslist
14. Set up an Etsy Storefront – Sell Personalized products
15. Freelance/Moonlight on platforms like Fiverr.com
16. Affiliate Marketing
17. **Direct Sales Reps:** Email your company name and referral links to: NancyGaskins.ECAmbassador@gmail.com. I will add a separate chapter for Direct Sales Affiliates: $25 each. Can be paid via paypal.com using the above email address.
18. Surprise Vacation Planner
19. Create a subscription-based business (product or service)
20. Write / Evaluate Resumes
21. Become a Notary
22. House Sitter
23. Wedding/Event Planner
24. Get Paid to Take Surveys, Watch TV & Play Games (Survey Junkie, InboxDollars)
25. Rent Your Guest Room: AirBnB
26. Host Themed Retreats
27. Become a Virtual Assistant
28. Disc Jockey / Karaoke Party

29. Become a Podcast Host and sell advertising
30. Flip Furniture
31. Proofread /Edit Term Papers, Manuscripts, Articles
32. Write and Publish a Book
33. Use your expertise to create a class, workshop, webinar, seminar, course, CD, or DVD you could sell online and offline
34. Coaching: Health, Fitness, Nutrition, Personal Finance, Life, Marriage, Career
35. BBQ Pork butts & ribs
36. Closet Organizer
37. Sell snacks at work
38. Build fishing rods, lures, flies
39. Photographer: Get creative! Set up a themed photo booth at special events and sell the digital copy or let them take a picture with their phones and charge a fee.
40. Gift wrapping for holidays
41. Personal Shopper
42. Walking Dogs
43. Mobile Pet Grooming
44. Sell on Poshmark and Mercari.
45. Swagbucks
46. Dog Sit
47. Thrifting and reselling. It takes a while to build, but you can do well with it.
48. Mystery shopper.
49. I do social media marketing and management from home
50. Babysit / Become a Nanny / Don't forget Eldercare
51. Teach with VIPKid
52. Tutor over Skype
53. Create Youtube Tutorials
54. Answer other people's questions (JustAnswer.com)
55. Read and Review Books Online: (theusreview.com)
56. Narrate Audiobooks
57. Get Paid To Listen To Music (musicxray.com)

58. Work from home travel agent
59. Typing/grammar skills? One of my side hustles is as a transcriptionist, and I really enjoy it.
60. Have a Garage Sale and Sell Stuff.
61. Are you a teacher? I've started designing and selling materials on TPT
62. Online boutique
63. I teach English to kids in China on PalFish. I tried VIP Kids and Gogokid but I don't have a teaching degree. PalFish doesn't require one. It's been great!
64. During the Fall and Winter months he builds and sells blanket ladders. They sell great at this time of year because they make a beautiful Christmas gift paired with a cozy blanket. We sell them for $30- it ends up being a pretty lucrative side hustle!
65. Digital Photography: Stock Photo Licensing
66. Paper quilled flowers, matted, framed and in a shadow box! Relaxing to make AND I can sell it!
67. Keepsake boxes out of flowers for weddings and funerals
68. Dress up characters for parties, celebrations and special occasions
69. House Cleaning
70. Janitorial Service For Businesses
71. Errand Service: groceries, doctors visits, hairdresser appointments, shuttle children (care.com, rover.com)
72. Pressure Washing Service
73. Teach CPR Classes
74. Painting Soffit Boards On Houses
75. Handyman (TaskRabbit.com)
76. Lawncare
77. Raking Leaves / Gutter Cleaning / Window Washing / Shoveling, Blowing Snow
78. Pool Cleaning
79. Washing & Detailing Cars
80. Run Facebook Ads for Businesses
81. Build Websites, Blogs, Sales Funnels

82. Graphic Design: Business cards, brochures, flyers
83. Local Tour Guide
84. Substitute Teach at your Local Schools
85. Start a Food Truck
86. Write Freelance Articles
87. Bookkeeping / Accounting Service
88. Tax Preparation
89. Music Lessons
90. Home Staging
91. Real Estate Agent
92. Referee Sports
93. Children's Entertainment
94. Custom Nutrition & Food Plans
95. Adult Education
96. Party Rental Equipment: Photo booths, slides, tents, bounce houses
97. Junk removal
98. Bicycle Assembly
99. Furniture Assembly
100. Handmade Goods: Sell at local craft fairs, flea markets, Etsy, Shopify.
    - Hand knit clothing and accessories
    - Upcycled vintage clothes
    - Dog sweaters and outfits
    - Pet collars and leashes
    - All kinds of bags
    - Screen printed shirts, tote bags
    - Throw pillows
    - Pottery
    - Patterns for knitting or sewing projects
    - Potted plants
    - Candles
    - Jams

- Pickled vegetables
- Fruit preserves
- Dog biscuits
- Dry pasta
- Sauces or soups
- Granola
- Chocolates and candy
- Jerky
- Tea blends
- Spice blends
- Essential oil blends
- Organic or natural skin care products
- Bath products
- Wood stools
- Coffee tables
- Lamps
- Jewelry
- Garden kits

101. Crafty Ideas:
- Corn hold boards
- Car air fresheners
- Christmas ornaments
- Hanging masks
- Children's bows
- Coaster sets
- Soap
- Custom dresses for girls
- Jewelry
- Custom drinkware
- Art
- Paint rocks
- Macramé
- Gnomes
- Headbands, scrunchies, washcloth scrubby
- Tie quilts
- Decorate cakes, cookies, cupcakes
- Crochet blankets, earmuffs
- Memory quilts from t-shirts, ties, pictures
- Pour paintings

IN PURSUIT OF THE AMERICAN DREAM

IN PURSUIT OF THE AMERICAN DREAM

DIRECT SALES WELCOME
BUSINESS DIRECTORY & SPONSORSHIP

This is Book 1 in a Planned 12-Month Book Series.

Business Owners & Entrepreneurs
Advertise your BUSINESS in the back of this book or an upcoming e-book and paperback edition for only $25 for a text ad, $50 for a business display ad.

Individuals & Businesses
Sponsorships are available for $35, which will include your photo, Name, City and State.

A separate Ramsey Financial Coach Directory will also be available in the back of each book for $50 each.

>Your Name
>Business Name
>Category
>Link
>Email or Telephone

This manuscript is updated on a weekly basis.
For immediate placement in the manuscript, send your payment via paypal.com to:
NancyGaskins.ECAmbassadors@gmail.com

Comments: Include the graphic and text content you want included.

IN PURSUIT OF THE AMERICAN DREAM

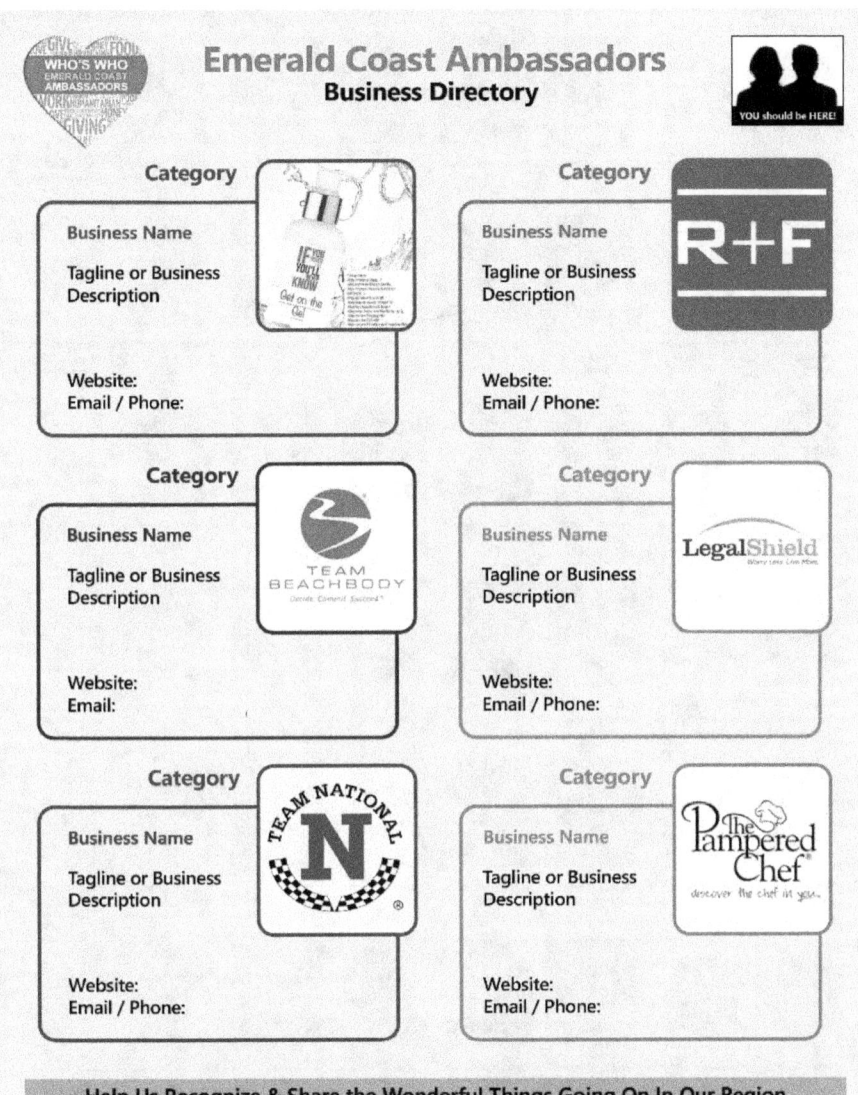

Display Ads: $50 each.

IN PURSUIT OF THE AMERICAN DREAM

Help us bring Financial Coaches and Financial Peace University Class Scholarships to Communities Across America

By becoming a Sponsor:

Your Picture, Name, City & State
$35 Each

Mission

Create a lifestyle where I will have enough time, money, health and fitness to do what I want, when I want, with those that mean the most.

Commitments

- Pursue an exciting, well-balanced life filled with purpose, achievement and financial prosperity; aspiring to live a life of excellence in both my personal and professional life.
- Live my life on purpose each day by investing my time, energy and resources on things that truly matter.
- Plan my work and work my plan so that I can achieve my goals and help others to do the same.
- Do what it takes to be healthy, look and feel fit, and to age well.
- Commit to living a highly successful personal and professional life; one that is pleasing to God and will inspire others to follow suit.
- Use my gifts, talents, experience, knowledge, skills, abilities and resources to make a significant difference in the lives of others; impacting my family, friends, neighborhood, workplace, community, nation, and the world in a positive manner.

Pledge

I agree to make a daily effort to live my life on purpose using the US Ambassadors for Prosperity, LLC Mission & Commitments Pledge as my guiding compass. I will encourage and inspire others to do the same.

NANCY GASKINS - EC AMBASSADOR
US Ambassadors For Prosperity
(850) 499-7149 | iTrainInvestors.com
NancyGaskins.ECAmbassador@gmail.com

ABOUT THE AUTHOR

Nancy Gaskins, MBA is an Emerald Coast Ambassador; creating, funding, supporting and participating in projects and organizations that make our region, nation and world a better place to live, work and play.

Nancy is a Serial Entrepreneur on a quest to make a world of difference and help others to do the same by sowing seeds of financial hope and entrepreneurial opportunity in communities across America.

Gaskins is a Speaker, Author, Newspaper Columnist, Radio Talk Show Host, Publisher, Community Volunteer and Philanthropist with over 20 years specializing in Entrepreneurship, Small Business Development, and Real Estate Investing.

Nancy has over 20 years of Sales, Marketing, and Senior Level Management Experience. Ms. Gaskins is a former Conference Event Planner, Director of Education, Dean, College Professor of Business, Corporate Controller and proud US Army spouse that has lived and worked in a variety of industries and capacities across the globe.

Nancy Gaskins received the President's Volunteer Service Award for her lifetime commitment to Community Service, the Heroine of the Infantryman's Shield of Sparta for her work supporting the Infantry Branch of the US Army, as well as numerous awards and recognition for her years of Community Service.

Now Available for Hire
- Keynote Speaker: Workshops, Seminars, Conferences, Retreats, & Special Events
- Consultation Options: Hourly, Weekly, Monthly, Quarterly
- Executive Board of Directors, Committee Member, Chairperson, Liaison
- Training & Development – Professional Development - Business Coaching
- Small Business Development - Grants For Startups - Startup Funding - Angel Investors

I look forward to hearing how the Dave Ramsey Baby Steps and Babystepper Community has impacted your life.

Feel free to email me your pictures, stories and advice to share with others who may be considering joining us on our journey or may just need a little encouragement.

Here's Some Ideas:

a. How did you raise the cash for baby step 1? How long did it take?
b. What are some of the setbacks (Murphy visits) you have experienced and how did you overcome them?
c. Tell us about your "get out of debt car," if you have (had) one.
d. Do you have a side gig? If so, tell us about it.
e. How long did it take you get to out of baby step 2? To become mortgage free (if applicable)
f. What's the dumbest thing you or someone you know has ever done with money?
g. Have you been the giver or recipient of outrageous generosity? Please share!
h. Anythig else you think would be beneficial to our readers.

Donation Information:

Donations of any amount are greatly appreciated. We are currently crowdfunding a perpetual grant fund that will provide a life enrichment resource library, scholarships for Ramsey Financial Coaches training and placement and Financial Peace University Classes for those who can't afford it.

Send your donation via Paypal.com to:
NancyGaskins.ECAmbassador@gmail.com
Your bank statement will read Jeremiah 2911 Ministries

IN PURSUIT OF THE AMERICAN DREAM

Nancy Gaskins Presents...
CROWD Funders Across AMERICA
Startup Grants

i Train Investors.com

★ SUPPORTER INFO ★

First Name: _____ Last Name: _____

Company Name (if applicable): _____

Address: _____

City: _____ State: _____ Zip: _____

Phone: (_____) _____ - _____

Email: _____ @ _____

Name of Person Who Referred You: _____

Signature: _____ Date: _____

SPONSORSHIP
[ ] $1,000 X ___ = $_____
[ ] Lump Sum OR
[ ] 4 Quarterly Payments
Royalty Reward: 23% | 10%

★ STATEMENT OF UNDERSTANDING ★

ALL campaign contributions are a GIFT, not an INVESTMENT. As a Supporter, I am eligible for Revenue Sharing Rewards. Every time one of our Sponsored Projects earns a dollar, a percentage is set aside as a REWARD for Project Supporters.

★ CAMPAIGN PLEDGE CONTRACT ★

Annual FINANCIAL Pledge
Registration: $65 Per Year PLUS
[ ] **Platinum:** $500 Lump Sum
[ ] **Gold:** $400 Paid $100 Quarterly
[ ] **Silver:** $200 Paid $ 50 Quarterly
[ ] **Bronze:** $120 Paid $ 30 Quarterly

Every 90-days, details for each Sponsored Project will be announced online, including the Revenue-Sharing Royalty Reward offered for each Project.

Revenue Sharing Rewards

Platinum: 45%   Silver: 20%
Gold: 30%   Bronze: 5%

NO Guarantees of Income Expressed or Implied.
Rewards will be distributed on the 10th of each month.

 (850) 499-7149   NancyGaskins.ECAmbassador@gmail.com   www.iTrainInvestors.com

www.ingramcontent.com/pod-product-compliance
Lightning Source LLC
Chambersburg PA
CBHW070653220526
45466CB00001B/419